DISABILITY STUDIES

REHABILITATION

INNOVATIONS AND CHALLENGES IN THE USE OF VIRTUAL REALITY TECHNOLOGIES

DISABILITY STUDIES

JOAV MERRICK - SERIES EDITOR -

MEDICAL DIRECTOR, MINISTRY OF SOCIAL AFFAIRS,
JERUSALEM, ISRAEL

Rehabilitation: Innovations and Challenges in the Use of Virtual Reality Technologies
Wendy Powell, Albert "Skip" Rizzo, Paul M. Sharkey and Joav Merrick, (Editors)
2017. ISBN: 978-1-53612-080-6

Pediatric Pain: Current Aspects
Hatim A. Omar, Dilip R. Patel, Donald E. Greydanus, and Joav Merrick (Editors)
2016. ISBN: 978-1-63485-505-1

Recent Advances on Using Virtual Reality Technologies for Rehabilitation
Paul M. Sharkey and Joav Merrick (Editors)
2016. ISBN: 978-1-63484-027-9

Technology, Rehabilitation and Empowerment of People with Special Needs
Lena Pareto, Paul M Sharkey and Joav Merrick (Editors)
2015. ISBN: 978-1-63482-713-3

Virtual Reality: Rehabilitation in Motor, Cognitive and Sensorial Disorders
Paul M. Sharkey and Joav Merrick (Editors)
2014. ISBN: 978-1-63321-773-7

Virtual Reality: People with Special Needs
Paul M. Sharkey and Joav Merrick (Editors)
2014. ISBN: 978-1-63321-729-4

Quality of Life and Intellectual Disability: Knowledge Application to other Social and Educational Challenges
Roy I. Brown and Rhonda M. Faragher (Editors)
2014. ISBN: 978-1-62948-264-4

Intellectual Disability: Some Current Issues
Joav Merrick, Donald E Greydanus and Dilip R. Patel (Editors)
2014. ISBN: 978-1-63321-855-0

From One Century to the Next: A History of Wrentham State School and the Institutional Model in Massachusetts
Ingrid Grenon
2014. ISBN: 978-1-63117-711-8 (Hardcover)
2014. ISBN: 978-1-63483-805-4 (Softcover)

Pain and the Elderly
Joav Merrick and Mimi M.Y. Tse
2013. ISBN: 978-1-62948-468-6

Pain: International Research in Pain Management
Joav Merrick, Patricia Schofield and Mohammed Morad (Editors)
2013. ISBN: 978-1-62948-423-5

Disability and Chronic Disease
Joav Merrick, Shoshana Aspler and Mohammed Morad (Editors)
2013. ISBN: 978-1-62948-288-0

Down Syndrome and Dementia. A Comprehensive and Historical Review
Vee P. Prasher
2012. ISBN: 978-1-62081-263-1

Rett Syndrome: Therapeutic Interventions
Meir Lotan and Joav Merrick (Editors)
2011. ISBN: 978-1-61728-614-8 (Hardcover)
2011. ISBN: 978-1-61728-080-1 (Softcover)

Pain Management Yearbook 2010
Joav Merrick (Editor)
2011. ISBN: 978-1-61209-972-9

Pain Management Yearbook 2009
Joav Merrick (Editor)
2011. ISBN: 978-1-61209-666-7

Pain. Brain Stimulation in the Treatment of Pain
Helena Knotkova, Ricardo Cruciani and Joav Merrick (Editors)
2011. ISBN: 978-1-60876-690-1

Neural Plasticity in Chronic Pain
Helena Knotkova, Ricardo A. Cruciani and Joav Merrick (Editors)
2011. ISBN: 978-1-61324-657-3

Disability from a Humanistic Perspective: Towards a Better Quality of Life
Shunit Reiter
2011. ISBN: 978-1-60456-412-9

Cancer in Children and Adults with Intellectual Disabilities: Current Research Aspects
Daniel Satgé and Joav Merrick (Editors)
2011. ISBN: 978-1-61761-856-7

Contemporary Issues in Intellectual Disabilities
V. P. Prasher
2010. ISBN: 978-1-61668-023-7

DISABILITY STUDIES

REHABILITATION

INNOVATIONS AND CHALLENGES IN THE USE OF VIRTUAL REALITY TECHNOLOGIES

WENDY POWELL
ALBERT "SKIP" RIZZO
PAUL M. SHARKEY
AND
JOAV MERRICK
EDITORS

nova science publishers
New York

Library of Congress Cataloging-in-Publication Data

ISBN: 978-1-53612-080-6

Published by Nova Science Publishers, Inc. † New York

CONTENTS

INTRODUCTION

In: Rehabilitation
Editors: Wendy Powell et al.
ISBN: 978-1-53612-080-6

Chapter 1

INNOVATIONS AND CHALLENGES IN THE USE OF VIRTUAL REALITY TECHNOLOGIES FOR REHABILITATION

Wendy A Powell[1,*], PhD, Albert A Rizzo[2], PhD, Paul M Sharkey[3], PhD and Joav Merrick[4-8], MD, MMedSci, DMSc

[1]School of Creative Technologies, University of Portsmouth, Winston Churchill Avenue, Portsmouth, United Kingdom
[2]Institute for Creative Technologies, University of Southern California, Los Angeles, US
[3]University of Reading, Reading, United Kingdom
[4]National Institute of Child Health and Human Development, Jerusalem, Israel
[5]Health Services, Division for Intellectual and Developmental Disabilities, Ministry of Social Affairs and Social Services, Jerusalem, Israel

* Correspondence: Wendy Powell PhD, Reader in Virtual Reality, School of Creative Technologies, University of Portsmouth, Winston Churchill Avenue, Portsmouth, United Kingdom. Email:wendy.powell@port.ac.uk.

[6]Department of Pediatrics, Mt Scopus Campus,
Hadassah Hebrew University Medical Center, Jerusalem, Israel
[7]Kentucky Children's Hospital, University of Kentucky,
Lexington, Kentucky, US
[8]Center for Healthy Development, School of Public Health,
Georgia State University, Atlanta, US

Virtual rehabilitation has been the focus of considerable research for many years, but the recent upsurge in consumer-ready virtual reality hardware and software has led to an increase in interest in its use in a variety of clinical and home settings. Balancing the upsurge in demand for innovative technological healthcare tools is the need for a credible evidence base for its use and guidance for practitioners on which systems and applications are suitable for different patient populations and rehabilitation goals. This promising branch of healthcare is already being used to benefit many patients in homes and clinics around the world, but it is evident that there is still much more to learn if we are to continue to push the boundaries of clinical innovation and excellence. In this book we present recent research addressing a number of these important topics, adding to our understanding of the complex issues and clinical considerations in virtual rehabilitation research and application.

INTRODUCTION

The use of virtual reality (VR) and associated technologies for health, wellbeing and support is a growing field, with an increasing body of expert knowledge and a wide range of potential application domains. Virtual rehabilitation has been the focus of considerable research for many years, but the recent upsurge in consumer-ready virtual reality hardware and software has led to an increase in interest in its use in a variety of clinical and home settings. Balancing the upsurge in demand for innovative technological healthcare tools is the need for a credible evidence base for its use and guidance for practitioners on which systems and applications are suitable for different patient populations and rehabilitation goals.

There is increasing evidence that virtual reality is a useful tool for a wide range of health conditions and clinical applications, including pain management, physical rehabilitation, treatment of anxiety disorders and post-traumatic stress, and many other physical, neurological and psychological conditions. However, it is important to bear in mind that these emerging technologies are not intended to replace the clinical expertise and human factors which are an integral part of the healthcare journey, but rather to provide a set of tools to supplement and support rehabilitation and to empower patients to participate in their own wellbeing. The complexity of this emerging area of healthcare should not be underestimated, with different patient groups requiring very different adaptations and interventions in order to achieve the desired outcomes. Fortunately, rigorous investigation and innovative development by practitioners working across the clinical, technical and human factors disciplines is improving our understanding, and supporting us to make better informed healthcare choices which optimise the benefits of this emerging technology.

A key area of concern is that of usability. Whilst this is of course important in any human-computer interaction, many patient populations present unique challenges, with cognitive or physical impairments rendering conventional interaction techniques impractical, and often requiring bespoke or customisable interfaces in order to translate the intent of the user into meaningful interaction. Innovative solutions include brain-computer interaction or gaze-directed selection for patients with significant paralysis, and partial hand support for gestural input post-stroke. Usability is of course not confined to the input techniques, but also the way in which content and feedback is presented to the user, which may require the use of iconography and audio prompts for users with learning disability or cognitive impairment, as well as the more conventional text based or visual cues. In addition, the acceptability of a system should also be considered, as a therapeutic intervention may be usable, but not necessarily something a patient or clinician would wish to engage with. For example, patients are often given home exercises using a mirror for retraining facial muscles after stroke, but compliance with this type of exercise can be poor (usable, but not necessarily acceptable). The use of VR technology can provide interactive feedback and gamification of the facial exercises, an approach which may be more acceptable to patients and lead to greater engagement with the therapeutic program.

Having designed a usable and engaging system appropriate to the target population, we come to the question of clinical efficacy - does it actually produce the desired outcomes? No matter how much a patient enjoys the virtual rehabilitation process, it is of little use unless it can be designed to elicit the desired behaviour leading to therapeutic gains. Studies which evaluate the way in which users interact and respond to feedback can give us valuable insights into both expected and unexpected ways in which users respond to the system, and the ability to tightly control almost every aspect of interaction with VR, and to monitor and record performance can provide data which not only allows us to monitor patient progress over time, but also leads to improve application design.

An additional benefit of technology-enhanced rehabilitation is the ability to individualise treatment programs dynamically, with either intelligent algorithms which respond to patient performance, or customisable programs which allow clinicians to create individualised treatment plans within the VR software.

Finally, the growing use of wearable devices allows us to harness additional physiological metrics such as breathing, heart rate or activity level during rehabilitation, even when it is carried out in a setting remote from the supervising practitioner, or in situations where intrusive monitoring is undesirable. This data can be streamed into the VR system and used to dynamically change the user experience, for example altering the level of fear stimulus in virtual reality exposure therapy in response to changing heart rate.

This promising branch of healthcare is already being used to benefit many patients in homes and clinics around the world, but it is evident that there is still much more to learn if we are to continue to push the boundaries of clinical innovation and excellence. In this book we present recent research addressing a number of these important topics, adding to our understanding of the complex issues and clinical considerations in virtual rehabilitation research and application.

SECTION ONE: VIRTUAL REHABILITATION

In: Rehabilitation
Editors: Wendy Powell et al.
ISBN: 978-1-53612-080-6

Chapter 2

CURRENT ISSUES AND CHALLENGES IN RESEARCH ON VIRTUAL REALITY THERAPY FOR CHILDREN WITH NEURODISABILITY

William J Farr[1,*], MA, DPhil,
Ian Male[1], MBBCH, MRCCP, MSc,
Dido Green[2], PhD, Christopher Morris[3], MSc, DPhil,
Heather Gage[5], Sarah Bailey[3], BSc(Hons), MPH, PhD,
Sandra Speller, MSc, GradDipPhys[1], MCSP,
Valerie Colville[4], MBA, Mandy Jackson[4],
Stephen Bremner[6], BSc, MSc, PhD
and Anjum Memon, MBBS, DPhil(Oxon), FFPH[6]

[1]Sussex Community NHS Foundation Trust, Brighton, West Sussex
[2]Department of Rehabilitation, Oxford Brookes University, Oxford
[3]Medical School, University of Exeter, Exeter
[4]Parent partnership advisors,
Sussex Community NHS Foundation Trust, Brighton

* Correspondence: William Farr, MA, DPhil, Senior Research Fellow in Paediatric Neurodisability, Sussex Community NHS Foundation Trust, Haywards Heath Health Clinic, Heath Road, West Sussex, RH16 3BB, United Kingdom. Email: will.farr@nhs.net.

[5]School of Economics, University of Surrey, Surrey
[6]Brighton and Sussex Medical School, Brighton, United Kingdom

A PICO (population, intervention, comparison, outcome) approach is adopted to discuss issues and challenges in virtual reality therapy research in community health settings. Widespread variation within and between populations, e.g., co-morbid conditions, complicates treatment fidelity and applicability. Interventions require flexible dose and frequency to fit into children's family circumstances, with clearly employed specialist paediatric research staff. Comparisons require adaptation to digital technology, and keep pace with development. Outcomes may overstate the impact of virtual reality therapy and technological novelty, while not fully unpacking hidden digital effects. A wide set of agreed, flexible, and patient-centred outcome measures are required to establish positive clinical baseline.

INTRODUCTION

"As a parent I know that my child, along with others, is keen to engage with modern technology in most aspects of life, from assisting with school work, communicating with others and as a form of entertainment. If physiotherapy was delivered using a "computer games" format, I feel that my child would be much keener to engage in undertaking necessary tasks and exercises" (parent of child with cerebral palsy).

Virtual reality therapy (VRT) has required a massive investment from academic and clinical researchers, from time taken to develop technology, getting clearance for using technology that may be commercially produced, piloting the work, grant applications, analysis of results and to rollout of interventions. There are a vast number of pitfalls that can affect the outcome and quality of intervention. There are a number of patterns that continually re-appear, and here we present those, in relation to children with neurodisability, so as to help future research. These issues – perhaps unsurprisingly – fit into problems associated with the population (including within this individual variation), intervention, comparison, and outcome (PICO). Problems occur because of the population we are studying, the intervention we employ, the way we try and compare groups, and the outcomes we are seeking. This paper will therefore look at: the population and variation that occurs across individuals within groups e.g., co-morbidity, as well as between groups (e.g., Autism versus Cerebral Palsy); the intervention – dose, frequency and therapist delivery; comparison issues within method construction – e.g., placebo, novelty effect; issues with outcome measures; their consistency, and how these are shaped by interaction with patient and public involvement (PPI) groups e.g., what parents tell us.

We use our own nationally (UK) funded feasibility study that looked at using the Nintendo Wii with children with Cerebral Palsy, outlined below, to ground our examples. We conclude with some pointers to tackle these problems.

FEASIBILITY OF VIRTUAL REALITY AS THERAPEUTIC INTERVENTION IN CHILDREN WITH AMBULATORY CEREBRAL PALSY

This study (National Institute of Health Research for Patient Benefit Programme PB-PG-0613-31046, approved by the Northwest-Lancaster National Health Service Research and Ethics Committee) looked at the feasibility of running a large-scale multi-centre study using the Nintendo Wii Fit to deliver regular home-based physiotherapy. Participating families completed a questionnaire regarding children's current use of computer games such as Nintendo Wii Fit within the home. Participating children were randomised into either a supported or unsupported (control) participant group. Supported participants followed a physiotherapist (PT) prescribed schedule over a 12-week period, utilising only specified Nintendo Wii Fit games for designated amounts of time per session. Sessions were recommended to last 30 minutes, three times a week with games selected for specific physiotherapy purposes, such as core stability or balance. During this 12-week period, fortnightly telephone contact to families oversaw the child's progress, updated game selection and responded to any queries in the PT supported group. The unsupported (control) participants were directed to use the Nintendo Wii Fit for 30-minute sessions, 3 times a week, over a 12-week period. However, they had free choice over which games they chose and duration each game was to be played within the session. Scheduled phone contact was minimal to this group during the 12-week period, unless specific physiotherapy advice was required. Carers and children of both groups were required to keep a simple daily diary to rate the sessions. Assessments of balance and functional mobility were taken before commencing the trial, halfway through, and on completion. An exit questionnaire asked parents and children to report on factors such as engagement, ease of use and effects of fatigue. Factors that impacted on the choice of method are discussed in section 3.

ISSUES AND CHALLENGES WITH THE POPULATION

Children with neurodisability present in a number of ways, from disorders affecting movement, such as cerebral palsy (CP), muscular dystrophy and developmental coordination disorder; to disorders of language and communication, including autistic spectrum disorder; to broader disorders of global development, such as is seen in children with Downs syndrome. To further complicate matters these conditions can co-occur, for example children on the autistic spectrum will commonly also have attention deficit hyperactivity disorder and developmental coordination disorder. Whilst for many children the cause of their disorder is uncertain, this is increasingly becoming identifiable, from known insults to the developing brain, including fetal alcohol syndrome, meningitis, extreme premature birth, hypoxic ischemic encephalopathy, to genetic and chromosomal disorders such as fragile X syndrome. In the UK, most children with neurodisability are seen at community based Child Development Centres (CDCs), often utilising home or school based therapeutic interventions. More complex cases may be seen in a small number of specialist tertiary centres, which are often hospital based. Furthermore, there is significant overlap between different diagnoses under the umbrella of neurodisability with children with CP at higher risk of social communication disorders and conversely, those on the autism spectrum being at high risk of movement impairments (1,2). At present, most neurodisability academic and research activity is based in the latter, begging the question of how to build a stronger research base in community centres aiming to improve practice in more common disorders (3).

Whilst there are pharmacological interventions that can help in some cases, for example the use of stimulant medication in attention deficit hyperactivity disorder, anticonvulsant medication in epilepsy, or the emerging use of gene splicing in Duchenne muscular dystrophy, it is rare for there to be a cure. Therefore, in most cases the mainstay of treatment is to ameliorate the impact of the condition through therapeutic intervention (3). Whilst programs of physiotherapy, occupational therapy, speech therapy or behaviour modification can all help, they often rely on parents or schools to deliver much of the program; from parental feedback this can result in significant stress within the family (4). Eventually this may well lead to the child refusing to complete their therapy. In the design stage of our study using the Wii Fit to determine whether it could improve balance and movement in children with cerebral palsy, parental input made it clear that as much as physical outcomes were important, for parents the primary measure of success of the intervention would be whether home based therapy could be delivered regularly without the levels of stress they associated with any attempt to deliver standard physiotherapy.

Each condition presents its own challenges to VRT research, although in many cases might be expected to respond to therapy developed through virtual reality technologies. For the current generation of children, virtual reality and information technology is a world they are very familiar and comfortable with, whether gaming, communicating, accessing information or working (5). It would not be surprising therefore if therapies delivered through virtual reality technologies should prove motivating for modern children. This is no more so than for children on the autistic spectrum, particularly those considered "high functioning", or diagnosed with Asperger's Syndrome, who are likely to be more comfortable interacting with technology than with their human peers, and indeed may well go on to work within the Information Technology industry (6). However, the challenges are very real.

Taking the example of autistic spectrum disorder, there is an immediate issue over the breadth of the spectrum, from a child who may be non-verbal with severe learning difficulties, to a "high functioning" child who may struggle understanding social interaction and be obsessive, yet at the same time have the genius to be a professor of maths, physics or computing, as portrayed in the TV character Sheldon Cooper (Big Bang Theory), or in Sherlock Holmes. As such, designing a study for children with Autistic Spectrum Disorder immediately presents the question of which children within the spectrum the intervention is aimed at. For example, we are currently developing a tool to support diagnostic assessment, incorporating a number of psychometric tests used in assessing school age children, into an App. We would anticipate that this is more likely to be helpful in children presenting at school age, and generally with a borderline to average academic ability, than those who are non-verbal and with severe learning difficulties.

Similarly, interventions for children with cerebral palsy, need to take account that this "blanket" term, describing children with movement disorders resulting from a static brain insult occurring during early development, may present with different types of abnormal movement including spasticity and ataxia, and with a wide range of severity, from a child with a mild hemiplegia with minimal effect on movement, to a child with whole body involvement who is wheelchair dependent. With our Wii study this raised the question of which children to target. We chose to focus on children who are able to walk and therefore hopefully use the Wii Fit without having to use supportive technologies, e.g., standing frame, to even stand on the Wii Fit.

Regardless of diagnosis, engagement in therapeutic intervention may prove problematic (4). In younger children, there may be issues over ability to access technologies, and to understand the research study enough to give assent. Teenagers by their nature may also choose to disengage, or may feel some Virtual Reality games are "no longer cool", and for younger children.

The individual conditions present their own difficulties, for example offering a group intervention for children on the autistic spectrum may be doomed to failure. Research on intervention effects in paediatric neurodisability has been confounded by a number of differing behavioural approaches and defining outcomes. In the UK, the James Lind Alliance - a leading charitable and academic think tank- recently determined the most important research questions in the field, helping set clearer agendas (3).

ISSUES AND CHALLENGES WITH THE INTERVENTION

Dose and frequency of an intervention employed in virtual rehabilitation is equally challenging, especially in community settings (7, 8). Community situations call for direct adaptations to family life, as emphasised in the International Classification of Functioning, Disability and Health – Children and Youth version (ICF-CY) where participation and activity performance across contexts is a key part of the framework (9). Acute settings e.g., hospitals can offer bespoke interventions but only in situ, whereas community settings are required to be more flexible in their approach to delivery of care. Therefore, whilst variation in the amount of time spent on a therapy varies dramatically across the literature, those that have positive results are often lacking the sample size to justify clinically important differences (10), and those studies with a sufficient sample size sometimes show little clinically significant impact (11). This is to be expected in a setting where social factors surrounding healthcare are equally as important as the treatment. A more personalised, adaptable, and consistent approach to treatment will only occur once VRT is adopted as regular care. Further, whilst VRT interventions are quite well classified (e.g., see 12), wider issues surrounding clinical research are more complex.

In our own present study, the intervention was developed using the Nintendo Wii Fit for use in the home for children with cerebral palsy. The Wii Fit was to be used three times a week, for thirty minutes, over a period of twelve weeks (e.g., see 13) using the Wii Fit Plus set of games. Early results suggest that 12 weeks is possibly too long a period of time for the intervention as many families reported having struggled to "fit in" the intervention. Children were often ill, tired from school, away on holiday, requiring treatment such as botulinum toxin, or were busy with a full and active life. Many parents also pointed to a tipping point in motivation around the 8th week, a time-point echoed in the earlier work of Deutsch et al. (14). After an active period of motivation, it appears that interventions may lose novelty to the participant, and return to being just another form of physiotherapy. Future work may need to employ more flexible methods to allow for time points where children are ill, or away, and not become lost or missing data, allowing the current status of a participant to alter according to personal circumstance (15).

The intervention was dependent on delivery and monitoring by therapists. In the local community setting, physiotherapists anecdotally had been using the Wii and the Wii Fit for many years, with focus groups developing programmes that were believed to target different areas of the body e.g., core strength, balance. Many physiotherapists were keen to become involved with the study but once the study was underway external pressures changed the landscape of delivery. Pressures on retention and recruitment of therapy staff reduced the time available, especially with an increased emphasis on delivering established clinical services. To that end, it seems imperative that specialist staff are employed where possible in a full-time research capacity to ensure clear protocol adherence, and ensure planned study recruitment and continuity. In England, research costs such as a research assessor measuring outcomes, are covered by the National Institute of Health Research (NIHR). Costs associated with delivering an intervention such as treatment are conversely met by local National Health Service (NHS) organisations. As a result, the tax funded NHS organisations may resist research that would involve the testing of innovative methods, especially if they take staff away from clinical services. To test new treatment methods, resources are therefore needed to 'backfill' staff so that specialist staff can be freed up to take part in research. Expecting regular staff to fit in research on top of regular daily clinical work does not work well in practice. To fully explore the impact of interventions with VRT the intervention needs to be run as if it were regular care, with fully employed clinical staff.

ISSUES AND CHALLENGES WITH APPROPRIATE COMPARISONS

Virtual rehabilitation and the use of new technology come with challenges to the creation of appropriate methods. A variety of models are already being attempted, such as 'micro-RCTs' (15), the use of standard controls (7), treatment as normal (16), reduced support in the intervention group (i.e., prescribed treatment versus freedom to use kit where appropriate) or even the use of computer controls such as delivery of an intervention via another modality such as a handheld device when an interactive console is being used in the experimental group (e.g., see 17). However, the underlying problem with new technology is that we do not know the impact of any hidden effects of technology. Hidden effects are well documented in discussions of the placebo effect within medical interventions (18-20) but there is yet to be a methodological discussion of the impact of digital technology on the participants - as well as researchers – behaviour (21). For example, what (if any) is the effect of the make or branding of technology and intuitive design if an iPhone is used compared to another standard smartphone? What technology, and what technological bias might already be present in the home? For example prior to our intervention in the home we conducted a survey of home use and presence of commercially available consoles. Parents and patients agreed that the most common, most useful tool, across all gradations of cerebral palsy, and especially for fine motor skills was the iPad (22). Therefore it is highly unlikely that individuals will have no experience of digital technology whatsoever, so there may be an impact of *prior experience*, plus an impact of *novelty* where an intervention uses a brand new piece of technology. Technological novelty may simply boost the interest in an intervention, thereby overstating its impact (23).

Ensuring health behaviour change, without lapses in the impact, is still relatively new and in development (24).

Furthermore, rate and pace at which research and development occurs is mismatched (25). This would be in keeping with Moore's law that predicts ever increasing memory expansion in technology (26). But there is a large disjuncture between the time it takes for research using new technological devices to occur, and the pace at which new devices are being produced, which means that it is difficult to validate devices and applications (25). In addition, a shortfall in the accuracy of sensors can further complicate technological use, reducing the reliability of clinically relevant information obtained from devices (27). Therefore it is imperative that any teams that use digital technology in clinical research keep abreast of the latest technological developments, with the right team in place. For example, the National Health Service in England sought to create and establish a database of smartphone applications in 2013 so that it could begin to ensure validity and compliance to local health ethics and ensure data protection to create a new endorsement model for patient focused healthcare applications. This pilot closed when research found though that 89% of applications were transmitting patient information to online services and without encrypted personal information (28). It is possible that some technology may still be more hype than hope (29)

During the creation of methods of intervention for digital technology use in clinical settings it is apparent that there are as yet many unanswered questions over the hidden impact of technology, and technology is set to become only ever more pervasive in our daily lives. Therefore the development of appropriate comparisons is still in its infancy. The lag from development to clinical research and validation is lengthy, as a result some authors have called for ever more close-knit research teams between the field of human-computer interaction and clinical research (23). In our own research, tensions existed between using technology that was fast becoming dated and used less by the general population (the Nintendo Wii has been surpassed by the Xbox in research), and establishing an effective and complex intervention that employed a technology when so little is known about hidden benefits and barriers. Agile, novel and new comparative methods will be needed as community based populations take part in digitally based technological interventions. Micro-RCTs are one possible solution, as is the use of similar interventions in wings of studies, but with subtle variants (e.g., more versus less support as in our own study), until more is known about the direct benefits of digital usage.

ISSUES AND CHALLENGES: RESULTS AND OUTCOME MEASURES

Our own systematic review of VRT for children with motor disorders confirmed the lack of fully powered studies to show if this is a valid direction of future travel, whether using off the shelf gaming technologies such as the Wii Fit, Xbox, iPad; or expensive, one off bespoke systems (30). Of the available studies in children with cerebral palsy, a couple of which included 20-30 children, most suggested some improvement in motor measures, with effect sizes of 0.3 to 0.8 (31,32) however there was little agreement over which outcome measures to use, even when focused on a specific skill such as balance. One study showed significant clinical improvement in dynamic balance and other motor outcomes in 10 children with Progressive Spinocerebellar Ataxia using the Xbox Kinect (31). This intervention was considered highly motivational and cost-efficient. Two studies gave promising results for the Wii Fit in children with developmental coordination disorder (16,34) including our own randomised control crossover pilot study based in a school setting, involving 19 children. Bruininks Oseretsky Test of Motor Proficiency Short Form (BOT-2), used as the main outcome, as a measure of improvement in motor coordination, improved in both groups during period of intervention, but fell close to baseline once the intervention finished (see figure one below for group 1 who had intervention first, followed by a control period). Further measures included Coordination Skills Questionnaire, a measure of the child's perception of their motor ability that also improved during intervention, but continued to do so even after intervention finished. Given that low self-esteem is such a common problem in children with Developmental Coordination Disorder, this may be as important as any actual improvement in motor coordination. The Strengths and Difficulties Questionnaire (SDQ), a measure of emotional wellbeing, was also included but few parents completed this following intervention. In those that did, scores improved significantly, often improving category from abnormal, or borderline, towards normal. This was particularly noticeable for the hyperactivity subscale.

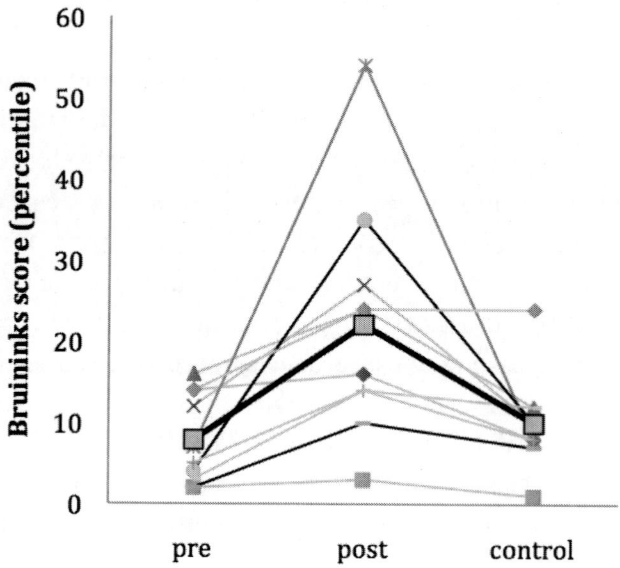

Figure 1. Change in BOT-2 percentile for individual children using the Wii Fit as a treatment for DCD in a school setting; group A in a crossover study received intervention initially and then acted as controls. Mean result shown by thickened black line.

Choice of outcome measure remains important. Yet even in an area such as motor disability, where instinctively clinical measurement should be relatively straight forward (at least compared to measuring, for example, changes in social function in children with autistic spectrum disorder), there is no clear agreement over which measures to use. One of the key questions in our current Wii Fit feasibility study with children with cerebral palsy has been to explore appropriateness of outcome measures. From a motor perspective one would instinctively expect the Wii Fit, as a glorified balance board, to improve measures of balance, of which we chose the BOT-2 and Timed Up and Go Test. The former was developed to determine motor proficiency and often used for children with Developmental Coordination Disorder where poor balance is a frequent problem. In such children the dominant side is tested for example in testing fine motor coordination-whereas we have had to adapt this in children with unilateral Cerebral Palsy to also test the affected side. The Gross Motor Function Measurement (GMFM), a specific measure of motor function for children with cerebral palsy has also been used. Although the study is still in progress, it is evident that for some children with very mild Cerebral Palsy, they reach 100% on the GMFM before completing the intervention (ceiling effect). We had concerns that BOT-2 might see the opposite (floor effect) with children scoring 0 pre-intervention. Some measures inevitably have ceiling or floor effects (e.g., Gross Motor Function Measure) when being used across a disorder that has a wide gradation, such as cerebral palsy as ranked by the Gross Motor Function Classification System.

The Goal Attainment Scale (GAS) has also demonstrated improvement in participating children, and mirrors clinical practice in therapeutic goal setting by personalising targets. However, goals set by each child will differ, so it is difficult to compare the degree of improvement in each child. Nevertheless, some of the individual stories of functional improvement are almost more persuasive of the benefits offered by VRT, than overall statistical analysis. For example, in this study one 12-year old boy improved from being unable to stand on one leg at all at the start of the study, to doing so successfully for 10 seconds by the end. Another 10-year old girl with hemiplegic cerebral palsy, involved in a one-week intensive pilot study using the Xbox Kinect for an hour a day for five days, focussing on upper limb function, reported with great excitement being able to do up her seatbelt for the first time in her life. As noted previously, measures of motor outcome are important to us as clinicians. However, for the family, impact of therapy on family life is an equally, or indeed, a more important outcome. For this study families have been encouraged to keep a diary exploring compliance with the protocol, but also to report difficulties in persuading the child to "do their exercises". The SDQ has also been used as a measure of emotional wellbeing for the child. Hopefully by the end of the study it will be clearer which measures are most useful, to inform future study design, with the need for larger, probably multi-centre RCTs, needed to finally confirm whether and how or VRT can provide a valid role within the therapeutic armoury for children with motor neurodisability. There is an equal need for similar feasibility studies in other areas of neurodisability, for example to explore the potential of collaborative play when using the Xbox Kinect adventure games to improve social skills in children with Autistic Spectrum Disorder.

The issue of individual variation – discussed in section 2 – results in a wide spread of scores which could be due to co-morbidity or wide gradation across a developmental disorder. One solution for evaluation is through multiple case studies analysis, thereby highlighting individual variation but isolating the impact on personal health (e.g., 35). For example, during a study week where we assessed the potential benefits of the Xbox Kinect for upper limb function, one patient struggled following instructions due to his additional learning needs, and attention deficit disorder. For example, whilst playing virtual bowling the child struggled to comprehend where the bowling ball went in space when the ball was virtually 'picked up'. On other tasks the child understood what to do but the notion of a 'virtual' ball was tricky to comprehend. Interestingly when the child was playing bowling on the Wii, demanding he hold and move the controller, it was much easier for him to grasp and use the ball with more proprioceptive feedback. His results therefore were not complete for the Xbox, but the outcome was useful in showing what he was capable of. Another child with cerebral palsy and autism, with oppositional defiant disorder, in the Wii Fit study, struggled to even get through any of the assessments with the physiotherapist. For the physiotherapist to be able to take any measurements a large amount of adaptation was used such as integrating other games into the session to ease the pressure on taking measurements. The child's parent eventually dropped out of that study due to stress when coming to clinic for assessment. While, this child presented without results at the end of the 12-week Wii fit study, information gained informed on study feasibility, in relation to age group, and the impact of co-morbid developmental disorders on the child's ability to adhere to measurement and study protocol.

CONCLUSIONS

We used a PICO (population, intervention, comparison, outcome) approach to discuss issues and challenges in virtual reality therapy research in community health settings. Future studies will need to be designed with sufficient power to prove, or disprove the effectiveness of VRT, and allow for children not completing studies, or consider excluding them from the onset if they are unlikely to complete. Therefore, unexpected results and outcomes are to be somewhat expected in the process of community research, and are ultimately more naturalistic to demonstrate how interventions would be employed in day-to-day life. Widespread variation exists within and between populations, complicating treatment fidelity and applicability; therefore necessitating care in sufficiently surveying populations with regards to technology (particularly access) before any intervention or experimentation takes place. Whilst traditional research methodologies, such as the gold standard Double Blind Randomised Placebo Controlled Trial, work well for example in studying a new medicine, the nature of Virtual Reality interventions within community settings makes this much harder to achieve. It will be important to learn the lessons of feasibility research such as described in this paper to enable studies that truly validate and hopefully justify the use of Virtual Reality Therapies in the future. Importantly, this would increase the evidence base underlying current practice in Paediatric Neurodisability.

ACKNOWLEDGMENTS

This project was funded by the National Institute for Health Research (Research for Patient Benefit Programme number: RfPB PB-PG-0613-

31046). The view and opinions expressed therein are those of the authors and do not necessarily reflect those of the RfPB NIHR programme, NIHR, NHS or the Department of Health.

REFERENCES

[1] Green D, Charman T, Pickles A, Chandler S, Loucas T, Simonoff E, et al. Impairment in movement skills of children with autistic spectrum disorders. Dev Med Child Neurol 2009;51(4):311-6.

[2] Christensen D, Van Naarden Braun K, Doernberg NS, Maenner MJ, Arneson CL, Durkin MS, et al. Prevalence of cerebral palsy, co-occurring autism spectrum disorders, and motor functioning –Autism and Developmental Disabilities Monitoring Network, USA, 2008. Dev Med Child Neurol 2014;56(1): 59-65.

[3] Morris C, Simkis D, Busk M, Morris M, Allard A, Denness J, et al. Setting research priorities to improve the health of children and young people with neurodisability: a British Academy of Childhood Disability-James Lind Alliance Research Priority Setting Partnership. BMJ Open 2015;5(1). doi:10.1136/bmjopen-2014-006233.

[4] Coombe S, Moore F, Bower E. A National Survey of the Amount of Physiotherapy Intervention Given to Children with Cerebral Palsy in the UK in the NHS. Assoc. Paed Chartered Physio 2012;3(1):5-18.

[5] Prensky M. Digital natives, digital immigrants. On Horizon 2001;9(5):1-6.

[6] Murray D, Lesser M, Dawson W. Attention, monotropism and the diagnostic criteria for autism. Autism 2005;9(2):139-56.

[7] James S, Ziviani J, Ware RS, Boyd R. Randomized controlled trial of web-based multimodal therapy for unilateral cerebral palsy to improve occupational performance. Dev Med Child Neurol 2015;57: 530-8.

[8] Boyd RN, Mitchell LE, James ST, Ziviani J, Sakzewski L, Smith A, et al. Move it to improve it (Mitii): study protocol of a randomised controlled trial of a novel web-based multimodal training program for children and adolescents with cerebral palsy. BMJ Open 2013;3(4). doi:10.1136/bmjopen-2012-002486.

[9] World Health Organisation. International classification of functioning, disability and health: Version for children and youth. Geneva, World Health Organisation, 2007.

[10] Tarakci D, Ozdincler AR, Tarakci E, Tutuncuoglu F, Ozmen M. Wii-based Balance Therapy to Imporve Balance Function of Children with Cerebral Palsy: A Pilot Study. J Phys Ther Sci 2013; 25:1123-7.

[11] Boyd RN, Baque E, Piovesana A, Ross S, Ziviani J, Sakzewski L, et al. Mitii™ ABI: study protocol of a randomised controlled trial of a web-based multi-modal training program for children and adolescents with an acquired brain injury (ABI). BMC Neurol 2015;15(1):1-29.

[12] Galvin J, Levac D. Facilitating clinical decision -making about the use of virtual reality within paediatric motor rehabilitation: describing and classifying virtual reality systems. Dev Neurorehabil 2011;14(2):112-22.

[13] Chen CL, Chen CY, Liaw MY, Chung CY, Wang CJ, Hong WH. Efficacy of home-based virtual cycling training on bone mineral density in ambulatory children with cerebral palsy. Osteoporos Int 2012;2012:1-8.

[14] Deutsch J, Borbely M, Filler J, Huhn K, Guarrera-Bowlby P. Use of a low-cost, commercially available gaming console (Wii) for rehabilitation of an adolescent with cerebral palsy. Phys Ther 2008;88(10): 1196-207.

[15] Dempsey W, Liao P, Klasnja P, Nahum-Shani I, Murphy SA. Randomised trials for the Fitbit generation. Signif 2015;2015:20-3.

[16] Ferguson GD, Jelsma D, Jelsma J, Smits-Engelsman BCM. The efficacy of two-task oriented interventions for children with developmental co-ordination disorder: Neuromotor task training and Nintendo Wii Fit training. Res Dev Disabil 2013;34(2013):2449-61.

[17] Hondori HM, Khademi M, Dodakian MA, McKenzie A, Lopes CV, Cramer SC. Choice of human-computer interaction mode in stroke rehabilitation. Neurorehabil Neural Repair 2015;30(3):258-65.

[18] Brissonnet J. Placebo, es-tu-la? Sci Pseudo Sciences 2011;294(1):38-48. [French]

[19] Brown WA. The placebo effect. Scientific Am 1998;1998:90-5.

[20] Moerman DE, Jonas WB. Deconstructing the placebo effect and finding the meaning response. Ann Int Med 2002;136(6):471-6.

[21] Farr W, Male I, Green D, Morris C, Gage H, Bailey S, et al. Methodological issues of using placebos in interventions based on digital technology. J Mob Tech Med, under review.

[22] Farr W, Male I, Speller S, Morris C, Green D, Bailey S, et al. A survey of home ownership and therapeutic use of commercially available consoles in children with cerebral palsy. Annu Sci Meeting BACCH, Leeds Beckett University, 2015.

[23] Zaczynski M. Efficacy before novelty: Establishing design guidelines in interactive gaming for rehabilitation and training. Graduate and postdoctoral affairs. Ottawa, Canada Carleton University; 2013.

[24] Klasjna P, Consolvo S, Pratt W. How to evaluate technologies for health behaviour change in HCI. CHI'11, Vancouver, BC, Canada, 2011 May 07-12.

[25] Pagoto S, Bennett GG. How behavioral science can advance digital health. Trans Behav Med 2013; 3:271-6.

[26] Moore GE. Cramming more components onto integrated circuits. Electronics 1965;1965:114-7.

[27] Steinberg D, Horwitz G, Zohar D. Building a business model in digital medicine. Nat Biotech 2015;33:910-20.

[28] Huckvale K, Tomas Prieto J, Tilney M, Benghozi P, Car J. Unaddressed privacy risks in accredited health and wellness apps: a cross-sectional systematic assessment. BMC Med 2015;13(214). doi: 10.1186/s12916-015-0444-y.

[29] Labrique A, Vasudevan L, Chang LW, Mehl G. H_pe for mHealth: More “y” or “o” on the horizon? Int J Med Inform 2013;82:467-9.

[30] Farr W, Male I. A meta-analysis of “Wii therapy” in children with cerebral palsy. Arch Dis Child 2013; 98(1):A97.

[31] Sharan D, Ajeesh P, Rameshkumar R, Mathankumar M, Jospin Paulina R, Manjula M. Virtual reality based therapy for post operative rehabilitation of children with cerebral palsy. J Work 2012;41(2012): 3612-5.

[32] Jelsma J, Pronk M, Ferguson G, Jelsma-Smit D. The effect of the Nintendo Wii Fit on balance control and gross motor function of children with spastic hemiplegic cerebral palsy. Dev Neurorehabil 2012; Digital early print 2012. doi: 10.3109/17518423.2012.711781.

[33] Ilg W, Schatton C, Schicks J, Giese M, Schols L, Synofzik M. Video game-based coordinative training improves ataxia in children with degenerative ataxia. Neurol 2012;79(20):2056-60.

[34] Hammond J, Jones V, Hill EL, Green D, Male I. An investigation of the impact of regular use of the Wii Fit to improve motor and psychosocial outcomes in children with movement difficulties: a pilot study. Child Care Health Dev 2013;40(2):165-75.

[35] Green D, Wilson P. Use of virtual reality in rehabilitation of movement in children with hemiplegia - A multiple case study evaluation. Disabil Rehabil 2012;34(7):593-604.

In: Rehabilitation
Editors: Wendy Powell et al.
ISBN: 978-1-53612-080-6

Chapter 3

PIRATE ADVENTURE AUTISM ASSESSMENT APP: A NEW TOOL TO AID CLINICAL ASSESSMENT OF CHILDREN WITH POSSIBLE AUTISTIC SPECTRUM DISORDER

Elizabeth Jordan*[1,*]*, BSc,
William J Farr*[1,2]*, DPhil, Stefan Fager*[3]*, MSc
***and Ian Male, MBBCH, MRCCP, MSc*[1,2]**
[1]Brighton and Sussex Medical School, University of Sussex, Brighton
[2]Mid Sussex Child Development Team,
Sussex Community NHS Foundation Trust,
Butlers Green Rd, Haywards Heath, W Sussex
[3]Cell Software Services, Frederick Terrace, Brighton, United Kingdom

Diagnostic assessment of possible Autistic Spectrum Disorder requires multidisciplinary assessment incorporating information from various settings, including psychometric assessment of the child. The Pirate

* *Correspondence:* William Farr, DPhil, Senior Research Fellow in Paediatric Neurodisability, Sussex Community NHS Foundation Trust, Haywards Heath Health Clinic, Heath Road, West Sussex, RH16 3BB, United Kingdom. Email: will.farr@nhs.net.

Adventure Autism Assessment software includes a number of psychometric tests adapted into a pirate adventure storyline. Early experience, presented here, suggests the tool is a useful adjunct to parental history and school questionnaire obtained at initial clinic, in determining the need for the child to proceed to a full, time consuming, expensive, diagnostic assessment.

Introduction

Autistic Spectrum Disorders (ASD) affect at least 1.1% of the population (1, 2) and could even be twice this figure allowing for possible under-representation in females. Affected children, or adults, would be expected to have difficulties in social interaction and communication particularly with their peer group, and repetitive and sensory behaviours, often described as "social communication difficulties." These difficulties can vary from a child with no speech who has minimal interaction with his peers, to a child who may be desperate to make friends but lacks the understanding as to how to do so, alongside obsessive interests.

In the absence of a diagnostic test, such as X-ray or blood test, a multidisciplinary assessment process is recommended in the UK and elsewhere (3, 4). This requires information being gathered from various places including home and educational settings, as well as observation and testing for evidence of autistic behaviours and/or patterns of thinking (5). A number of tools have been developed to aid this process including formal structured history tools such as the Autism Diagnostic Interview (ADI-R) and the Diagnostic Interview for Social Communication Disorders (DISCO), and observational tools such as the Autism Diagnostic Observation Schedule (ADOS) and the NEuroPSYchological developmental assessment (NEPSY). However, NICE recognises: "no single tool alone seems to have adequate sensitivity and specificity for diagnosis of autism" (6).

Current interactive methods including software tools such as 'Autism and Beyond' do not fulfil clinical need (7) and formal tools such as ADOS (8), and Autism Spectrum Disorder Observation for Children (9) take over an hour to complete. The multidisciplinary process takes a long time. Our own study of practice in UK based Child Development Centres suggests this takes around 13 hours of professional time to complete, costing around £800 per child (10). We also identified that most teams (10-12) employ a 2-stage process (see Figure 1) including an initial "stage one" screening, or general developmental clinic, which typically lasts 60-90 minutes (cost £100). This is often carried out by a paediatrician working alone, where a decision is made about whether to proceed to the full multidisciplinary diagnostic assessment (5). At this initial clinic, the clinician may have access to information from validated screening questionnaires such as the Social Communication Questionnaire (SCQ) (11) giving a parental perspective of the child, and information from an educational setting (often also in questionnaire form). However, the clinician largely relies on taking a broad developmental history from the parents/carer and observing the child in clinic. A full "Stage Two" diagnostic assessment may include a paediatrician, a speech therapist and clinical psychologist and others, using formal history taking which specifically addresses the presence of autistic symptoms and also formal observational assessment for signs of autism, and may include observation and discussion in the child's educational setting.

The combination of this lengthy process and a steady increase in referrals, has placed diagnostic services under increasing pressure resulting in the waiting time for a complete assessment in the UK taking as long as 6 months to 2 years (12). In the UK the "number of [autism] referrals has increased to a level greater than one would expect based on national prevalence" (13) while what is required is a "more responsive environment of diagnosis and support" (13). Experience has been similar in US and Australia resulting in a single practitioner approach being accepted for many children, although it is acknowledged this is not ideal (3, 4). Any approach that can ease pressure on diagnostic pathways, for example by improving decision making at initial Stage One assessment, has the potential to improve the quality and speed of the patient journey through the system and potentially even to reduce costs.

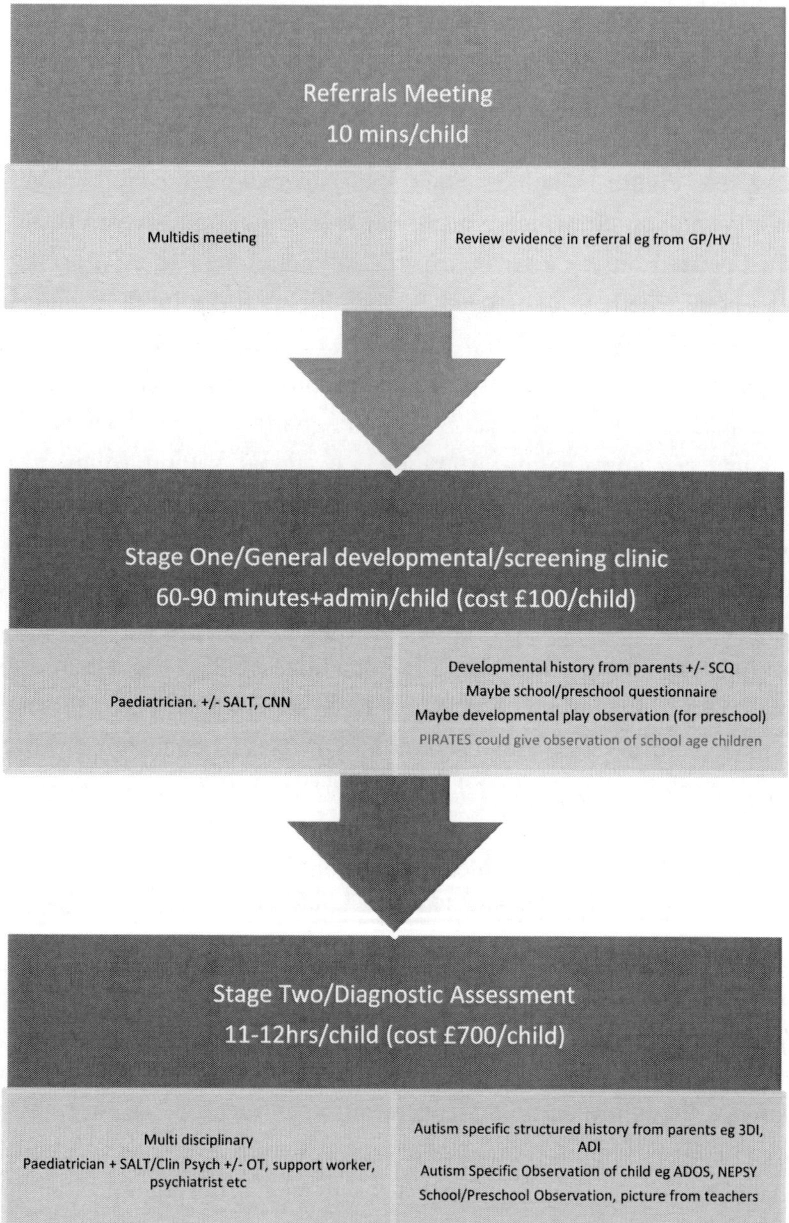

Figure 1. Typical UK 2 Stage ASD Diagnostic Pathway, demonstrating where Pirates could be used.

This chapter presents a computer based tool, developed by the research team, which early clinical experience suggests could provide additional information to the initial assessment. When used as an adjunct to current clinical practice, this could create a more detailed picture of the child, and inform decision making over the need for a full diagnostic assessment.

THE PIRATE SOFTWARE

The initial inspiration behind the Pirate Adventure Autism Assessment App (Pirates) concept was a toy pirate ship in the child development clinic. The toy pirates were used in developmental play assessment of the child using a story line based on the Sally Anne Test (14), a well-established test exploring the child's ability to know what someone else is thinking (Theory of Mind or ToM), thought to still be central to Autistic thinking following the longitudinal SIBS studies (15). In the original Sally Anne Test, two dolls, Sally and Anne, hide a toy. Anne then goes away, and whilst she is away, Sally hides the toy somewhere else. When Anne returns the child is asked where Anne will look for the toy. A child with typical theory of mind should be able to realise that Anne does not know the toy was moved and therefore will look where she helped Sally to hide the toy originally. We replaced Sally and Anne with two pirates, and the toy with treasure, which appeared to engage the child's interest, the majority of whom are boys, and contributed to the picture of the child. Sometimes unexpected extra information emerged, for example one child objected to the use of a single coin commenting: "that's not treasure," demonstrating a pedantic response typical of a child with Asperger's syndrome. Another child demonstrated a higher order of theory of mind, helping to exclude an ASD diagnosis, commenting that whilst the returning pirate would expect the treasure to be where he helped to hide it originally, he might look "elsewhere if he thought the other pirate was untrustworthy." Around the same time we discovered Lego Mini-figures, including a range of pirates. These are produced with a wide range of facial expressions, offering the possibility of creating scenarios matching tests of recognition of facial expression (affect recognition), another common area of weakness in children with ASD. With this in mind we conducted a detailed review of the literature underpinning psychometric assessment of children with possible ASD, and around how to design ASD friendly apps.

LITERATURE REVIEW

A literature search was conducted using the PsycINFO database using the search terms "autism AND (screening OR diagnostic)" to explore available diagnostic and screening tools, yielding 39 relevant studies. A similar search was conducted on current clinical trials databases, and exploring the "app store" for autism diagnostic tools. Current clinical practice and the role of diagnostic tools such as the ADOS and NEPSY were also observed. The review also covered the original literature of psychological theories underpinning current testing including Theory of Mind, False Belief Tests, Affect Recognition and Francesca Happe's "Strange Stories." Storyboards which have subsequently been built into the tool were constructed incorporating identified tests, adapted into the context of a pirate adventure story line. This included tests of affect recognition (e.g., see 16), including the ability to match facial expressions (see Figure 1), identify appropriate situational facial expression (e.g., "how does the captain feel about being made to walk the plank?"), and short-term recall of facial expression. We also included First Order Theory of Mind tests, adapting the "unexpected contents (Smarties tube) task" (see figure 2) and Sally Ann tests, and Second Order Theory of Mind tests (17). The "Strange Stories" exploring the child's ability to recognise and explain the use of sarcasm and a lie (18), were added, alongside idiom, such as "the treasure cost him an arm and a leg" (19).

Design heuristics for software to engage children on the autistic spectrum included factors such as text should be concise, literal and unambiguous, readable and avoiding capitalising whole sentences. Navigation should be clear, e.g., using tap or swipe with clear prompts e.g., buttons or arrows. Buttons should be large and finger friendly. Design features included: uncluttered layout, engaging format and story line, clear feedback (e.g., progress bar), visual images, simple colour palette avoiding black text on white background (visually over stimulating), using easily readable font such as Sans Serif, no time restrictions and no penalising ("errorless learning"), avoiding flashing, fast animations (avoiding sensory overload), abrupt changes, whilst using prompting and reinforcement (20).

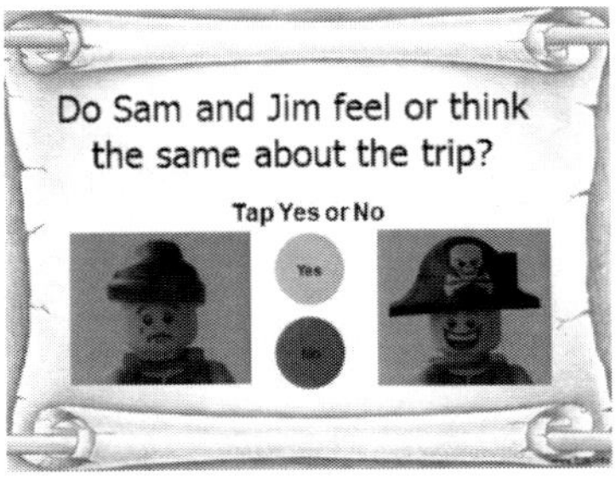

Figure 2. Example of affect recognition slide.

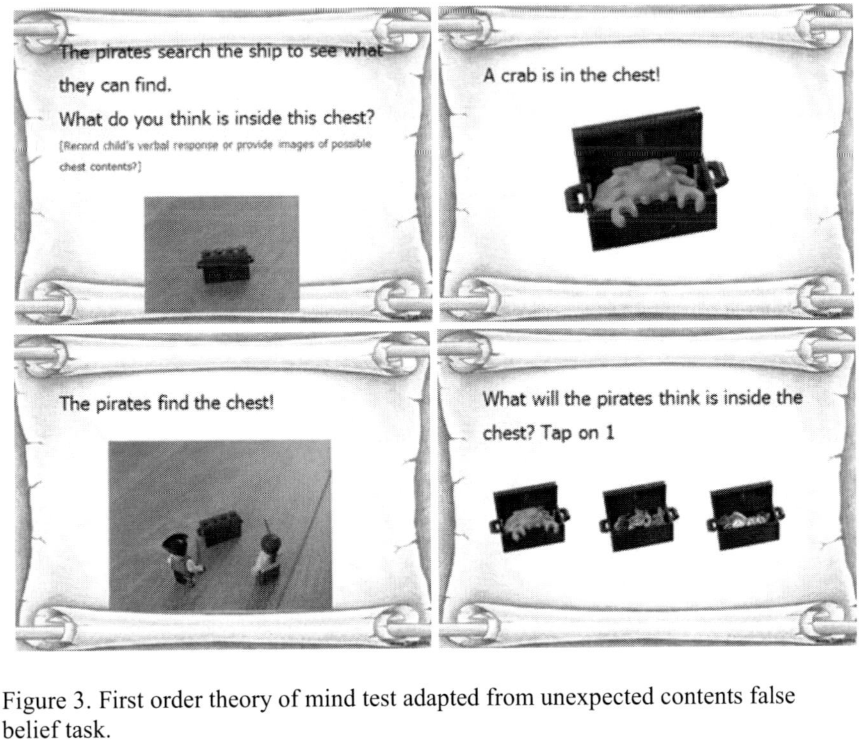

Figure 3. First order theory of mind test adapted from unexpected contents false belief task.

The resulting scenarios were built into a sequential pirate adventure story line, although most of these can be used as stand-alone tests. The initial PowerPoint and subsequent Apple IOS/Windows versions have incorporated the recommended design features, for example having a Flesh-Reading Ease score of 93.7 (0 unreadable, 100 most readable), use of ellipses, as often used in comics, between slides to maintain suspense, use of a progress bar and touch/tap buttons and Sans Serif.

EARLY CLINICAL EXPERIENCE

The app has been piloted by paediatric consultants working in three local Child Development Centres, two at initial appointment, in one at a diagnostic clinic. Results, including correct/incorrect responses, and the child's interaction with the tool and clinician, are currently recorded in paper format whilst adherence to medical device regulation and data protection is completed. Feedback from the consultants and parents has been positive in many cases. Clinicians state that the software helps in creating a picture of the child. Results from individual tests has emerged that give additional information such as how the child interacts with the clinician, for example one child commented as the clinician expressed surprise at there being a crab in the treasure chest "are you afraid of crabs?", misinterpreting the clinician's emotions and facial expression. This software mirrors observational information obtained in a full diagnostic assessment using tools such as ADOS and NEPSY, which can take 1-2 hours to complete, whilst the software takes on average 10 minutes to complete, successfully fitting into a standard 60-90 minute clinical appointment. When the software is used in combination with parental history and information from the child's educational setting this helps in deciding whether the child needs to proceed to full diagnostic assessment, or even in reaching a diagnostic conclusion, as a result. Parents like the fact that the doctor has been seen to "do a test for autism" and engage in observing their child's ability either to perform tests correctly (which can help in reassuring the parents) or to struggle, suggesting further assessment is required. Most children engage with the familiarity of the Lego Mini-figures, when offered the opportunity of playing on a computer/iPad, and with the pirate theme e.g., consultants commented that it was helpful having an observational tool to use with school aged children, mirroring use of observation of early development and play used in clinic with pre-school children.

Two children demonstrate the potential benefits that might be achieved. The first, a 6-year-old boy was referred by school due to significant concerns about social communication. Parental history was cautious, coupled with a low parent completed SCQ score of only 3, a close to average score. He incorrectly answered questions on affect recognition, false belief (crab), lie, sarcasm and idiom. Therefore a decision was made to pursue diagnostic assessment based on the level of concern expressed by school, whilst seeing his performance on Pirates helped his parents accept this was appropriate. At his subsequent diagnostic assessment ASD was confirmed. The second example, a 7-year-old girl, had originally been assessed whilst at pre-school although a diagnosis was not confirmed as parental history was unclear. Over time, her parents became more aware of her difficulties in school, raising increasing concerns about the widening social gap with her peers. She struggled with affect recognition, false belief, and ToM testing, lie, sarcasm, and idiom. ASD was confirmed following a school visit by the clinical team's speech therapist. However had Pirates been validated for use it was felt diagnosis could have been given at the initial meeting as parental concerns (including an SCQ score of 22), the school description, and psychometric test results offered by Pirates were all very suggestive of a diagnosis.

DISCUSSION AND CONCLUSION

Whilst this paper reports very early results, it is encouraging that clinicians experienced in assessing children with possible ASD, have reported very positive experiences around its use. The tool appears to provide information about the child's patterns of thinking; equivalent to psychometric testing used in full diagnostic assessment, and when used together with parental history and school questionnaire can help give a more complete picture of the child when deciding whether to proceed to diagnostic assessment. Parent feedback has also been very encouraging, one parent even asking if she could purchase the app to help teach her child to recognise different facial expressions. Initial impressions suggest a good correlation between performance on the tool and the presence of symptoms of possible ASD from parental history and school questionnaire. Further studies are needed to assess the performance of typically developing children, and whether this alters with age. This needs to be compared with performance in children with known ASD, and other conditions such as language disorder and learning difficulties that present with symptoms similar to children on the autistic spectrum. It will be important to ascertain, for example, whether there are different performance patterns in the different diagnostic groups, such as specific weaknesses in language based tests in children with language disorder. This early experience, along with discussion with experts in psychological testing for children, has highlighted a couple of areas that would benefit from adaptation, for example in modifying the storyline used to test the child's level of understanding of tasks to record the nature of the child's interaction with the game and clinician for second order theory of mind. The software may also benefit from the addition of a clinical observational checklist. Use of video of child-clinician interaction may be incorporated allowing the clinical assessment to be reviewed. Overall, our early experience suggests that the tablet-based tool could become a useful adjunct to initial assessment of children referred with possible ASD.

REFERENCES

[1] Baird G, Simonoff E, Pickles A, Chandler S, Loucas T, Meldrum D, et al. Prevalence of disorders of the autism spectrum in a population cohort of children in South Thames: the Special Needs and Autism Project (SNAP). Lancet 2006;368:210-5.

[2] Frieden TR, Jaffe HW, Cono, J, Richards CL, Iademarco MF. Prevalance of autism spectrum disorder among children aged 8 years, Autism and Developmental Monitoring Network, 11 sites, United States, 2012. MMWR Surveill Summ 2014;63(2):1-24.

[3] Plauche Johnson C, Myers S. Identification and evluation of children with autism spectrum disorders. Pediatrics 2007;120:2007-2361 DOI: 10.1542/peds.2007-2361.

[4] Taylor L, Brown P, Eapen V, Harris A, Maybery M, Midford S, et al. Autism spectrum disorder diagnosis in Australia: Are we meeting best practice standards? Brisbane: Autism Co-operative Research Centre, 2016.

[5] NICE. Autism diagnosis in children and young people: Recognition, referral and diagnosis in children and young people on the autism spectrum. London: National Institute for Health and Care Excellence, 2011.

[6] NICE. Autism diagnosis in children and young people. London: National Institute for Health and Care Excellence, 2013.

[7] Autism and beyond. URL: https://autismandbeyond.researchkit.duke.edu/study

[8] Lord C, Rutter M, DiLavore PC, Risi S, Gotham K, Bishop S. Autism Diagnostic Observation Schedule, second edition (ADOS-2) manual (Part I): Modules 1-4. Torrance, CA: Western Psychological Services, 2012.

[9] Neale D, Matson J, Hattier M. Validity of the Autism Spectrum Disorder Observation for Children (ASD-OC). J Ment Health Res Intellect Disabil 2014;7(1).

[10] Galliver M, Gowling E, Farr W, Gain A, Male I. How much does it cost the UK National Health Service to assess a child with possible Autism? In preparation.

[11] Rutter M, Bailey A, Lord C. The Social Communication Questionnaire. Los Angeles, CA: Western Psychological Services, 2003.

[12] Autism Achieve Alliance. Autism spectrum disorders: Waiting for assessment. Executive Summary. Autism Achieve Alliance, 2014.

[13] Hansard online. URL: www.parliament.uk 8th march 2016 https://hansard.parliament.uk/Commons/2016-03-08/debates/16030851000002/AutismDiagnosisWaitingTimes.

[14] Baron-Cohen S, Leslie AM, Frith U. Does the autistic child have a "theory of mind"? Cognition 1985;21: 37-46.

[15] Chawarska K, Shic F, Macari S, Campbell D, Brian J, Landa R, et al. 18-month predictors of later outcomes in younger siblings of children with autism spectrum disorder: A baby siblings research consortium study. J Am Acad Child Adolesc Psychiatry 2014;53(12):1317-27.

[16] Golan O, Ashwin E, Granader Y, McClintock S, Day K, Leggett V, et al. Enhancing emotion recognition in children with autism spectrum conditions: an intervention using animated vehicles with real emotional faces. Autism 2010;40(3):269-79.

[17] Perner J, Wimmer H. 'John thinks that Mary thinks that . . .': Attribution of second order beliefs by 5- to 10-year-old children. J Exp Child Psychol 1985;39:437-71.

[18] Happé FGE. An advanced test of theory of mind: Understanding of story characters' thoughts and feelings by able autistic, mentally handicapped, and normal children and adults. Autism 1994;24(2):129-54.

[19] Barton M. It's raining cats and dogs: an autism guide to the confusing world of idioms, metaphors and everyday expressions, London: Jessica Kingsley, 2012.

[20] Fletcher-Watson S. Evidence-based technology design and commercialisation: Recommendations derived from research in education and autism. TechTrends 2015;59(1):84-8.

In: Rehabilitation
Editors: Wendy Powell et al.
ISBN: 978-1-53612-080-6

Chapter 4

HOME BASED VIRTUAL REHABILITATION FOR UPPER EXTREMITY FUNCTIONAL RECOVERY POST-STROKE

Qinyin Qiu**, PhD, Amanda Cronce,
Gerald Fluet, PT, DPT, PhD, Jigna Patel, PT,
Alma Merians, PT, PhD and Sergei Adamovich, PhD
Department of Rehabilitation and Movement Sciences,
Rutgers University, Newark, New Jersey, US
Department of Biomedical Engineering,
New Jersey Institute of Technology, University Heights,
Newark, New Jersey, US

After stroke, sustained hand rehabilitation training is required for continuous improvement and maintenance of distal function. An ideal home-based telerehabilitation system has to be low cost, easy to set up, effective in motivating the user to use it every day, generate progress reports to the user for self-tracking, and provide daily monitoring to remote clinicians. In this chapter, we present a system designed and implemented

* Correspondence: Qinyin Qiu, PhD, Department of Rehabilitation and Movement Sciences, Rutgers University, 65 Bergen Street, Newark, NJ, United States. Email: qiuqinyin@gmail.com.

in our lab: the NJIT Home-based Virtual Rehabilitation System (NJIT HoVRS). A single subject proof of concept study was conducted and demonstrated that this system is easy to access and effective in motivating subjects to train at home.

INTRODUCTION

Stroke remains the leading cause of serious, long-term disability in the United States, with over 6.8 million stroke survivors (1). Although the incidence of death from stroke has been decreasing due to new medical treatments during the acute episode, this still leaves a significant number of individuals permanently disabled. Only 10% of survivors recover completely, the majority have a long-term or lifelong need for help to perform activities of daily living and require further rehabilitation (2) as a result of a significant brain injury. Deficits in motor control affect the stroke survivors' capacity for independent living and economic self-sufficiency. The impact of even mild to moderate deficits in hand control in particular, affect many activities of daily living.

Intensity and progression have been proposed as key factors in successful stroke rehabilitation. A very recent article, offering a theoretical framework with which to develop future post-stroke clinical trials, proposed that intensity and progression are the active ingredients of a rehabilitation program that drive neural plasticity and lead to positive functional outcomes (3). Studies have shown that sustained hand rehabilitation training is important for continuous improvement and maintenance of function (4, 5). If the amount of therapy is critical to rehabilitation, our current institutional limitations undermine the probabilities for successful outcomes. Time constraints and expensive personnel as well as the restricted length of stay in both acute care hospitals and rehabilitation restrain the provision of an adequate dose of training for persons with stroke. After discharge from the inpatient stay, access to rehabilitation therapy can be difficult for some patients. This is due in part to inadequate insurance, lack of transportation, and the patient's dependence on their caregiver. Having access to long-term rehabilitation training anywhere and at any time is necessary for sub-acute and chronic patients to continuously improve their functional abilities. There is a momentum building for increased attention to the development of technological interventions intended to support repetitive on-going home-based practice for better recovery of upper extremity motor function.

Innovative telerehabilitation systems have been developed using information and communication technologies to provide rehabilitation services at a distance. Many studies have developed video-game driven systems from commercially available gaming consoles such as Wii and Microsoft Kinect (6). Other groups have examined the use of custom-made tele-rehabilitation systems (7, 8). Most of these systems target arm or postural control, and require more space than may be available in the patient's home. These systems do not address hand rehabilitation. There is a vital need to explore intensive home-based upper extremity interventions that focus on the hand. An ideal home-based telerehabilitation system has to be low cost, easy to setup, able to motivate the user to use it every day, generate progress reports to the user for self-tracking, and provide daily monitoring to remote clinicians. Exciting new technologies have now made this approach possible and hold promise for long-term benefit. These technological advances - for the first time - allow for virtual reality simulations interfaced with discrete finger and hand tracking that is affordable and easy to use.

The NJIT Home-based Virtual Rehabilitation System (NJIT HoVRS) integrates the Leap Motion Controller and virtual reality technology to provide focused rehabilitation of wrist, hand, and finger movement. This paper presents the design concepts behind the NJIT HoVRS and the results of a proof of concept test. We believe that the NJIT HoVRS is a powerful tool that will give patients access to affordable, effective, and long-term rehabilitation in their home, allowing them to maximize and sustain stroke recovery, while increasing their overall quality of life.

SYSTEM DESIGN

NJIT HoVRS has two sub-systems to deliver home-based training: 1) a patient based platform to provide the training and 2) a server based online data logging and reporting system. In the patient's home, a cross platform virtual reality training application runs video games (developed in the Unity 3D game engine using the language C#) on their home computer. The Leap Motion Controller (LMC) infrared tracking device is used to capture motion of the hand and arm movement without requiring wearable sensors that may be difficult to put on independently or could potentially restrain movement.

Hardware

The Leap Motion Controller (LMC) (see Figure 1) is a $50 computer hardware sensor that captures detailed hand movement as well as hand gestures. The heart of the device consists of two cameras and three infrared LEDs. A data validation study showed the LMC to be accurate and reliable as long as the target is within its visual area (±250 mm of the LCM center) (9). The device's USB controller reads the sensor data into its own local memory and performs any necessary resolution adjustments. This data is then streamed via USB to the Leap Motion image API. From there, we programmed the system to feed tracking data into virtual reality activities by calling the Leap Motion API.

If the patient's arm is severely impaired and he/she cannot support the hand against gravity above the Leap Motion Controller, the Armon™ Edero, a spring compensation system, can be provided to the subject (see Figure 1). The Edero provides 12 different levels of passive support allowing it to accommodate a wide range of patient sizes and strength levels. It requires a single, setting that can be provided during the patient's initial evaluation. Minimal instruction is required to teach patients to readjust support levels on their own

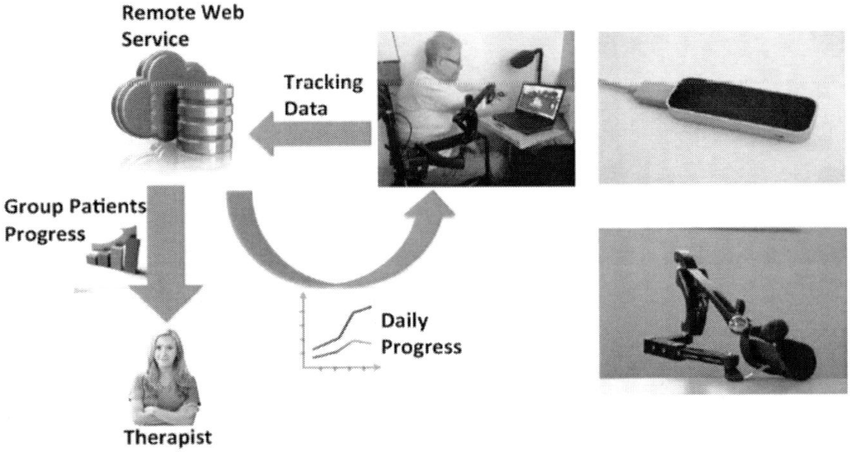

Figure 1. Left: RAVR-Home architecture design. Upper right: Leap Motion Controller. Lower Right: Armon Edero™ arm support.

Figure 2. Left: RAVR-Home architecture design. Upper right: Leap Motion Controller. Lower Right: Armon Edero™ arm support. Figure 2. a: Maze, b. Whack-A-Mole, c. Soccer Goalie, d. Bowling, e. Fruit Picking, f. Fruit Catching, g. Car game, h. Hand Fly, i. Wrist Fly, j. Arm Fly, k. Piano, l. Breakout.

Software

A user-friendly GUI interface lists all of the training activities allowing patients to choose which activity they want to begin with using just one mouse click.

Currently twelve games have been developed, each one designed to focus on training a specific hand or arm movement such as wrist rotation or finger individuation (see Figure 2). An avatar is at the corner of all game environments to provide verbal praise and encouragement as therapists usually do in real world. Therapists configuration page can be enabled by pressing "T" for game condition pre-setup, such as work space size, game challenge level, etc (see Figure 3a). All games are downloadable via HoVRS website.

Maze: Player controls the movement of the virtual character through their hand location. The score is defined by the number of spheres the character intercepts along the maze path. The character falls if he deviates from the defined path. As the game level increases in difficulty; the platforms and bridges that the character is guided over become narrower and sharp turns become more frequent.

Whack-a-mole: The player controls the position of the hammer through arm movement in the horizontal plane. Rotation of the hammer is controlled by pronation/supination. Success score is defined by the amount of moles hit.

Soccer goalie: The player controls the position of the virtual hand to block the approaching soccer balls from hitting the goal.

Bowling: The player reaches forward and extends their fingers to apply force to the ball to knock over the pins.

Fruit picking: The player must reach and use a pinch movement with their thumb and forefinger to pick apples and oranges from trees and sort them into the correct basket to increase the score.

Fruit catching: To catch the fruit, the player controls location of a collection basket through horizontal arm movement. To increase the score, the player uses forearm pronation/supination to drop the collected fruit into a second basket. The frequency of falling fruit decreases when the player misses 25% of the falling fruit

Car game: The player practices opening and closing their hand to control the car speed. Closing the hand slows the car down allowing it to maneuver over speed bumps.

Hand flying: The plane speed is constant. The player controls vertical position of the plane by opening and closing their hand. Success score is defined by the number of floating spheres intercepted.

Wrist flying: The plane speed is constant. The player controls vertical position of the plane by changing the pitch of their hand at the wrist. Success score is defined by the number of floating spheres intercepted.

Arm flying: The plane speed is constant. The player controls the horizontal position and roll of the plane by moving their arm left and right and pronating/supinating their forearm. Success score is defined by the number of floating spheres intercepted.

Piano: The player plays a song by pressing the highlighted key with the indicated virtual finger. The amount of finger individuation required to successfully press any keys increases as the player progresses. However, it scales back down when they are unable to hit the key for 6 seconds.

Breakout: The paddle used to direct the ball follows the palm position of the player. The ball is directed by bouncing off the paddle and hitting the bricks above to clear the screen.

Figure 3. a. Therapist setup interface; b. Calibration interface; c. Hand not visible warning.

System calibration and hand position correction

A comprehensive calibration procedure (see Figure 3b) is used to measure each subject's active range of motion within the LMC visual area and this range is scaled to fit into the video game virtual environment. To create greater ease of use, games have been designed to display a red frame (see Figure 3c) to guide the subject back to the LMC visual area whenever his/her hand deviates from the calibrated range.

Data collection

Performance and kinematic data collected during rehabilitation training using the NJIT HoVRS is securely transferred to Amazon Simple Storage Service (S3) at the end of the each training session for offline analysis. Patient data is automatically processed to produce daily progress reports. Therapists can securely access the reports through a password protected website, which will also host system updates.

SYSTEM VALIDATION

In order to evaluate NJIT HoVRS' ease of use and reliability, a 45 year old female patient with moderate hemiparesis of the upper extremity (UEFMA = 45) due to a cortical stroke was recruited. She was a police detective prior to the stroke and was able to return to full time deskwork 6 months after the event. She lives alone but her family lives nearby and gave her a lot of support during her rehabilitation. She had little to no video game experience prior to this training. The system was placed in her home. Without help from the therapist or engineer, she successfully finished 7 thirty minutes training sessions utilizing all twelve of the games at least twice (Figure 4).

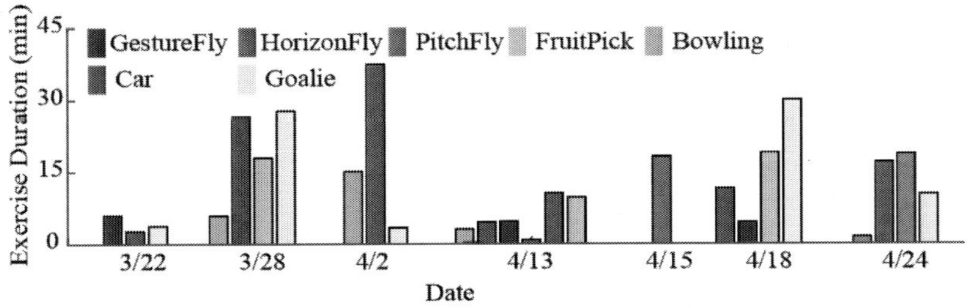

Figure 4. Exercise duration for each gaming activity over one month of therapy, as reported by the HoVRS website.

Car simulation

As shown in Figure 5 (left panel), the subject was able to maintain her hand above the Leap Motion and control virtual car speed by opening and closing her hand. As the simulation went on, she gradually opened her hand more than she was capable of during the initial calibration.

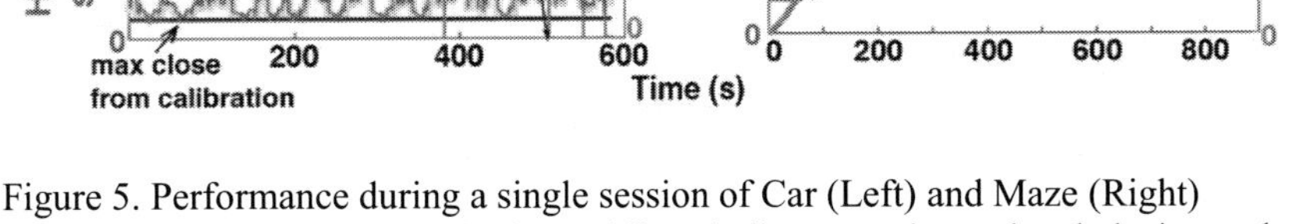

Figure 5. Performance during a single session of Car (Left) and Maze (Right) simulations. Left panel: Two horizontal lines indicate maximum hand closing and opening during initial calibration. Arrow indicates moment when hand tracking was lost and the car speed dropped to zero. Right panel: Arrow indicates moment when the avatar fell off the maze plane and the game restarted at the beginning of the level.3

Maze simulation

In the maze simulation (Figure 5, right panel), after successfully reaching the target, the subject will advance to a higher level that requires more hand stability. If the subject fails to reach the target, the score collected from the current level will be deducted and the subject starts again from the beginning of the current level. As shown in Figure 5 right, our subject was able to successfully pass the first four easy levels. However, as difficulty level increased, the subject started to slow down and make multiple attempts to complete fifth level.

Questionnaire

In a post-training questionnaire, the subject noted the system's ease of use and a desire to incorporate the system as part of her on-going therapy. Subject felt that this therapy system was engaging. In her comments, she said that the system is easy to use, and she almost forgot that she was participating in rehabilitation training while she was focusing on trying to complete the computer tasks. Her arm was tired after doing the training, but not her hand. She felt this system would improve her hand motion. She wished it could have been part of her original therapy and wanted it to be part of her on-going therapy. Subject said most of the games were engaging. She was able to understand the requirements and learn how to play them quickly. The easiest game for her was the Car simulation because it had a one-dimensional control requiring only hand opening and closing to manipulate the car's speed. Her favorite game was the Arm Flying simulation because its soothing music made her relax and enjoy the training. The most difficult game for her was the piano because it required both arm stability and finger individuation. The most confusing game was Whack-A-Mole because different lighting and random appearance of the moles provided too much information and caused confusion about how to proceed. The most non-intuitive game was Soccer Goalie because the orientation of the virtual hand and the real hand did not match. The virtual hand displayed in the virtual environment was vertical with the palm facing forward, while the real hand was horizontal with the palm facing down.

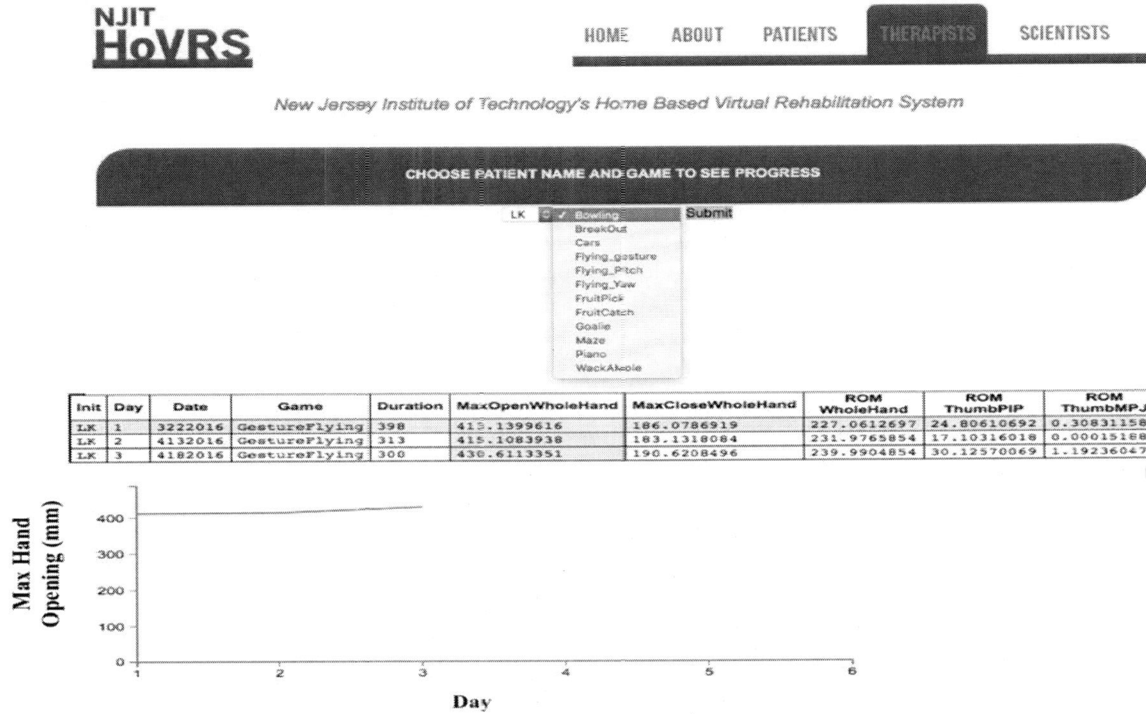

Init	Day	Date	Game	Duration	MaxOpenWholeHand	MaxCloseWholeHand	ROM WholeHand	ROM ThumbPIP	ROM ThumbMPJ
LK	1	3222016	GestureFlying	398	413.1399616	186.0786919	227.0612697	24.80610692	0.308311581
LK	2	4132016	GestureFlying	313	415.1083938	183.1318084	231.9765854	17.10316018	0.000151885
LK	3	4182016	GestureFlying	300	430.6113351	190.6208496	239.9904854	30.12570069	1.192360472

Figure 6. Therapist can monitor subject's daily progress via HoVRS website. Plot shows the sum of distances between the palm and five fingertips.

System server for data monitoring and visualization

All training data could be accessed remotely from the data server via HoVRS website. The therapist can access daily training data of a specific subject for a specific game activity via website. As shown in Figure 6, therapist chose to display daily maximum hand opening value from game GestureFly on website. The therapist sent a short text messages to the patient whenever there was new training data shown on the server side as a way to praise her effort and encourage continued participation. The data showed that repeated performance of several simulations resulted in increased finger opening as measured by the system.

DISCUSSION

We intend to bring a "wellness" approach to the achievement of independent upper extremity manipulation and function for people post-stroke. The National Wellness Institute (mailto: http://www.national wellness.org) encourages "a conscious, self-directed and evolving process of achieving full potential." Through the development of an easy to use and engaging home-based virtual reality exercise program we modeled the wellness concept of continual self-directed exercise to allow people with hand and upper extremity motor deficits to achieve their full potential. NJIT HoVRS is a low cost, easy to setup, reliable and engaging home-based hand rehabilitation system. Virtual reality simulations are engaging and the subject was motivated to play them for a long period of time. Currently, there is little available for home-based hand therapy (10). The advantage of this home-based system is its focus on hand-based simulations. Our objective was to provide markerless hand tracking (LEAP) and simple support of arm motion in 3-dimensional space to allow the patient to move freely, while it helps them keep their hands over the LEAP's effective range. Clear online directions, delivered visually and aurally through imaginative avatars allow the individuals to practice independently. Novel algorithms provide safe and effective interactions with the serious games. Despite this complexity, the use of novel technologies makes this affordable system easy to use. Compliance with home-based exercise programs is low. We believe strongly that the NJIT-HoVRS home-based system will effectively deal with compliance issues through the engaging games, the easy to use system (no donning and doffing difficulties), the enticing encouraging avatars, the success algorithms and the instant availability of daily achievement graphs. This self-paced, independent home practice is consistent with a "wellness" approach that should empower stroke survivors to take an active self-directed approach to their rehabilitation.

REFERENCES

[1] Go AS, Mozaffarian D, Roger VL. Heart disease and stroke statistics. 2014 update: a report from the American Heart Association. Circulation 2014;129:e28-e292.

[2] Centers for Disease Control and Prevention (CDC). Outpatient rehabilitation among stroke survivors—21 States and the District of Columbia, 2005. MMWR 2007;56(20):504-7.

[3] Bowden MG, Woodbury ML, Duncan PW. Promoting neuroplasticity and recovery after stroke: future directions for rehabilitation clinical trials. Curr Opin Neurol 2013;26(1):37-42.

[4] Hodics T, Cohen LG, Cramer SC. Functional imaging of intervention effects in stroke motor rehabilitation, Arch Phys Med Rehabil 2006;87(12 Supl 2):36-42.

[5] Page SJ, Gater DR, and Bach-Y-Rita P. Reconsidering the motor recovery plateau in stroke rehabilitation, Arch Phys Med Rehabil 2004;85(8):1377-81.

[6] Metcalf CD, Robinson R, Malpass AJ. Markerless motion capture and measurement of hand kinematics: validation and application to home-based upper limb rehabilitation. IEEE Trans Biomed Eng 2013; 60:2184–92.

[7] Adamovich SV, Merians A, Boian R, Tremaine M, Burdea G, Recce M, et al. Virtual reality based system for hand rehabilitation post-stroke. Presence 2005;14:161-74.

[8] Turolla A, Daud Albasini QA, Oboe R, Agostini M, Tonin P, Paolucci S, et al. Haptic-based neurorehabilitation in poststroke patients: a feasibility prospective multicentre trial for robotics hand rehabilitation. Comput Math Methods Med 2013;2013:895492. doi.org/10.1155/2013/895492.

[9] Guna J, Jakus G, Pogačnik M, Tomažič S, Sodnik J. An analysis of the precision and reliability of the leap motion sensor and its suitability for static and dynamic tracking. Sensors 2014;14:3702-20.

[10] Hayward KS, Neibling BA, Barker RN. Self-administered, home-based SMART (sensorimotor active rehabilitation training) arm training: A single-case report. Am J Occup Ther 2015;69(4):6904210020p1-8. Doi: 10.5014/ajot.2015.01055.

In: Rehabilitation
Editors: Wendy Powell et al.
ISBN: 978-1-53612-080-6

Chapter 5

AUTOMATED INSTRUCTIONS AND REAL TIME FEEDBACK FOR UPPER LIMB COMPUTERIZED MIRROR THERAPY WITH AUGMENTED REFLECTION TECHNOLOGY

Jack Pinches, BSc(Hons)
and Simon Hoermann*, BSc, MSc, PhD
Department of Information Science and Department of Medicine,
University of Otago, University of Otago, Dunedin, New Zealand
School of Electrical and Information Engineering,
The University of Sydney, Sydney, Australia

The use of virtual and augmented reality (VR/AR) in physical rehabilitation can provide better control, improved user motivation, and flexibility in how therapy is offered. Mirror therapy is a therapeutic intervention that has been shown to be beneficial for upper limb stroke rehabilitation. This chapter presents an AR mirror therapy system that provides automatic instructions and feedback. A within-subjects design

---

* Correspondence: Simon Hoermann, Research Associate, Positive Computing Laboratory, School of Electrical and Information Engineering, The University of Sydney, Sydney, Australia. Email: simon.hoermann@sydney.edu.au.

user study with healthy volunteers was conducted to evaluate the usability, perceived suitability, satisfaction, general experience and participants' performance and preference. We compared two conditions where the system automatically instructed the participants and (i) where the system additionally provided feedback, or (ii) the system did not provide feedback. All participants were able to complete the automated mirror therapy intervention. Participants significantly rated the usability and suitability of the automated intervention as positive. The comparisons between the two conditions on *user experience* and *satisfaction* indicated preferences for the feedback condition; however it was not statistically significant. In the direct comparison between systems, participants showed a strong and significant preference for the feedback condition. A few participants reported a mild level of discomfort attributed to the sitting position, exercises and placement of their hands on the table. With this study, further progress towards an automated system for the provision of mirror therapy was achieved and successfully evaluated with healthy participants. Preparations for clinical evaluations using this automated system with patients suffering from motor impairments after stroke can now commence.

INTRODUCTION

Computer mediated visual feedback systems using virtual reality and augmented reality such as Augmented Reflection Technology (ART) show promising potential as part of a rehabilitation program for motor impairments after a stroke, to improve arm function and assist in daily living (1).

Despite the availability of many protocols for stroke rehabilitation and intervention, today only about 10% of stroke patients recover completely, while 25% will suffer from minor impairments, 40% will experience moderate to severe impairments that require special care, 10% will require care in a nursing home or long term care facility, and 15% will die shortly after (2).

An emerging possibility to improve the therapeutic outcomes of stroke rehabilitation is the use of technology such as ART. ART uses computer mediated visual feedback to provide an alternative to traditional therapeutic methods (3). An ART system consists of two monitors connected to a single computer, with one monitor for the patient and one for the therapist. The patient's hand movements are captured by web camera(s), the captured video is processed and manipulated by software and the results are displayed on the patient screen. This approach allows for a variety of computer mediated therapeutic interventions. ART has been clinically evaluated as part of an upper limb stroke rehabilitation scheme and a specifically tailored protocol for the intervention was established (4).

This tailored protocol is based on a validated therapeutic intervention called mirror therapy (MT). During MT, a mirror is placed between limbs with the mirror facing the unimpaired side; patients can see a visual overlay of their unimpaired hand at their impaired side. The therapeutic effects of MT are speculated to be due to increased activation in brain areas (e.g., precuneus, posterior cingulate cortex) functionally connected to the stroke affected area in the motor cortex (5, 6). MT was originally proposed as an intervention to manage phantom limb pain (7). However, its efficacy as a therapeutic intervention for motor rehabilitation after stroke was soon after investigated (8) and was recently confirmed in a systematic review and meta-analysis (9).

In MT with ART, computer manipulated visualisations of the patient's hand(s) are shown on screen. The unimpaired hand is mirrored to the other side of the screen to give the patients the impression of actually using their impaired hand. Patients are verbally instructed by a therapist to carry out exercises (hand movements) from a predefined category depending on the stage of the therapy. The therapist has to be present to provide verbal instruction and feedback to the patients.

A systematic review to explore the requirements of autonomous training for adults was conducted by Jettkowski, Morkisch and Dohle (10). They found that many principles of motor rehabilitation such as intensive and active execution of exercises, relevance of exercises to daily activities, adequate selection of exercises and consideration of the context can be integrated into autonomous training. However, providing feedback during therapy was not achievable without the presence of a therapist. Nevertheless, the use of technology to provide feedback was suggested as a possible solution.

This research project extends the existing ART system with the functionality to: a) automatically generate instructions for the user to carry out therapeutic exercises as prescribed in the MT protocol for ART and b) to provide automatic feedback during the therapy session. The viability of the computer generated instructions to allow unsupervised execution of the therapeutic exercises was evaluated, as well as how automatic real-time feedback affected the exercise execution and user experience.

A user study was conducted with healthy participants. The study combined quantitative and qualitative measures to determine user performance and experience. Validated questionnaires were used alongside a semi-structured interview at the end of the experiment. This research contributes towards current stroke rehabilitation approaches by evaluating the effectiveness of automatic feedback in an autonomous computer mediated therapy scenario. This research will help with the refinement of how computer generated feedback can be used in therapeutic applications, and how the addition of feedback causes a change in user performance and experience. The possibility to provide an enhanced therapeutic experience could lead to higher levels of patient motivation and therefore positively contribute to the efficiency and effectiveness of therapy (11). In addition, the findings on the viability of the computer generated instructions can inform the use and development of therapeutic systems for unsupervised autonomous use by patients either at home or in a clinical context.

SYSTEM

The system used consisted of three main components: 1) An off-the-shelf webcam with a HD 720p RGB image sensor (Creative Senz3D, Creative Technology Ltd), 2) tailor-made software to process the image data using OpenCV from the webcam and deliver to the application, and lastly 3) the application itself created using Unity3D which provides the environment in which users will interact with and see on screen. In addition, another screen was used by the experimenter to start and stop the application and configure the various settings.

The hardware of the system consisted of a monitor (Dell Widescreen Full-HD 22” Monitor) mounted on a monitor arm attached to the desk. The arm allows for users to place their hands under the monitor. The webcam was mounted on a stand attached to the monitor arm and was pointed towards the area where users place their hands. The desktop was covered with a blue curtain placed behind the monitor and under the webcam, to be used as part of the background subtraction performed on the camera image data. A detailed description of how the ART system is used can be found in Hoermann et al. (4).

Interaction Capture

To display only the hands of a user on screen, background subtraction was performed on each frame of the webcam stream. The colour image was converted from RGB colour space to HSV. Each pixel was checked to ensure that the hue was within a predetermined range which represented the colour blue. If the pixels were within this range, they were set to transparent. This left the pixels which represented the hands, which were set as opaque.

The reason for using the colour blue was because of the contrast it provides to the skin colour. The placement of the blue fabric in the interaction supports the subtraction of everything but the hands.

Instructions

The system provided instructions by displaying an image of the current exercise on the screen on the same side as the hand (see figure 1). The pixels in that image that represented the hand were semi-transparent so that the user was still able see their own hand when they overlapped, and all other pixels were completely transparent.

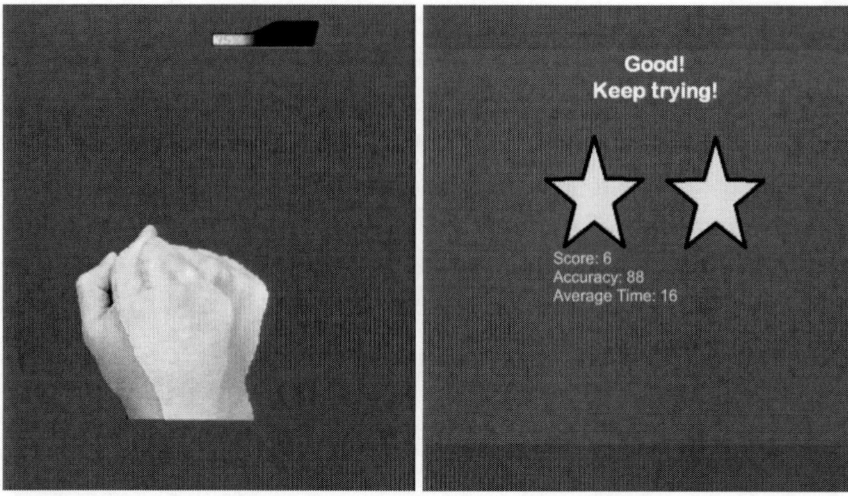

Figure 1. The half-transparent image of the exercise and the actual hand of the user (left), post-phase feedback (right).

If the user was able to complete an exercise, another exercise was randomly selected from a list of specific exercises without consecutive repetitions of the same exercise. When a new exercise was displayed, a short audio clip was played to inform the user.

Evaluation

The current exercise is displayed on screen for a user to follow, while another image of the same exercise is also used by the system for comparison with the images from the video-stream of the actual user's hand. This comparison image is exactly the same as the displayed image except that the transparent pixels are set to black. The system then performs a count of the non-black pixels of the image, which gives a quantitative value for how much space the exercise occupies. This value is referred to as the maximum accuracy for that exercise. When the system performs the background segmentation of the camera data, it also checks the pixels against the corresponding pixels of the comparison image. If this check finds that there are pixels in the camera data that are not empty and also pixels in the image that are not empty, it then assumes that a user has their hand in an area where the exercise is being displayed.

When pixels are found where expected then an accuracy score is incremented, and if non empty pixels are found in the camera data where there are empty pixels, the score is decremented. This approximates how well a user is matching the exercise. The current accuracy score is constantly updated, and then calculated to determine the percentage it is of the total. This percentage is used as the input for the real-time feedback bar (see Figure 1, left, right upper corner).

The evaluation of an exercise is done in two steps: first the accuracy score must be above the pre-set threshold, and second the user must maintain this accuracy above the threshold for a pre-set time. If at any point the accuracy drops below the threshold, then the hold time timer is reset and will start once the threshold is reached again. The threshold and hold time are read in from an eXtensible Markup Language (XML) file at system start and can be changed to a custom value to meet required performance. Data is automatically saved into an XML file for each user. The threshold value used for the user study was 80% and the hold time 3 seconds. This means a user must maintain a hand shape at 80% or above similarity to the reference image for 3 consecutive seconds to progress to the next exercise.

Feedback

The feedback bar (Figure 1, left image, upper right corner) displays the accuracy score in real-time, and states the percentage currently achieved. When an exercise is completed, this accuracy score is saved into the user's XML file, along with the time taken to complete the exercise as well as the exercise ID.

When a phase is completed, the performance information is used to evaluate user performance. The current evaluation method is based on the average accuracy score, which will fit into one of three levels, each indicating an increasing level. The levels are calculated by: 100 minus threshold divided by three. The chosen feedback is then displayed on the screen, on the same side of the screen where the hand is displayed. There is a different feedback screen for each of the three levels, each displaying the number of stars to represent the feedback level achieved and a motivational message. Additionally, performance data from the phase is displayed, showing the score: number of completed exercises, average accuracy, and average completion time. The threshold value used in the experiment is 80, hence an average accuracy of 80 to 86.7 would result in one-star feedback, 86.7 to 93.3 in two stars and above 93.3 in three stars.

USER STUDY

Participants

Twenty-eight participants were recruited from the University of Otago and Dunedin area. The sample consisted of 20 males and 8 females working in a range of disciplines, between the ages of 21 and 62 years with an average age of 33.79 (*SD* = 12.96). All participants reported to have normal vision and no impairments that could affect their performance during the experiment. Twenty-four participants were right-handed, two left handed and two ambidextrous as measured with the Edinburgh Handedness Inventory (12). All participants provided written informed consent and received a chocolate bar as compensation for their time.

Measures

The experience questionnaire consisted of questions taken from a Mixed Reality Experience questionnaire (13), and was filled out six times, once after each phase was completed. The questions asked participants to rate the ease of performing the exercises, their performance, performance satisfaction, motivation, concentration, and enjoyment. The rating-scale ranged from 0 to 10.

After each condition, participants completed a satisfaction questionnaire, which was a subset (questions 1, 2, 3, 4, 6, 7, 10, 11, 16, and 17) of an IBM Usability Satisfaction Questionnaire (14). This questionnaire comprised of ten questions on a rating-scale of 1 to 9, on how participants felt about the system while performing the task and the task itself.

Once both conditions had been completed, three different questionnaires were used. The first was a suitability questionnaire containing fourteen questions specifically related to virtual rehabilitation systems (15). The response-scale was increased from the original 5-point scale to a scale ranging from −5 to 5. The second questionnaire was a usability questionnaire to evaluate the perceived usability (16). The final questionnaire contained four self-created questions asking participants to pick between each condition on a scale of −2 to 2 for their overall preference, ease of use, motivation, and concentration.

Design

The experiment used a within subject design, with the 28 participants pre-randomised and counter-balanced for the feedback and non-feedback conditions, and for the hand used in the experiment. The hand used in the experiment was randomly predetermined and hand dominance was not taken into account but was recorded as part of the demographic questionnaire. The independent variable was "feedback" with levels (i) system will give feedback and (ii) no feedback is provided by the system. In both conditions the instructions were provided automatically by the system. The dependent variables were participant satisfaction, motivation, enjoyment, concentration, and perceived usability. The performance data collected was the exercise execution time, exercise accuracy, and score.

Procedure

Experiments were conducted in a controlled lab environment to reduce unnecessary distraction for the participants. Two conditions were evaluated: MT with automated instruction and feedback, and MT with automated instruction but without feedback.

Upon arrival, participants were greeted and given an information sheet detailing the experiment and what they should expect. After reading this, they were presented with a consent form to give their formal written consent. Participants were asked to complete a demographic questionnaire once they had consented to taking part in the experiment.

Before starting with the conditions, an initial setup step was required. This involved the experimenter verbally guiding the participant through the exercises and using the ART system to capture a photo of the participant's hand for each exercise. The 16 hand movements used were the same as used in a previous study (4) and were based on the Mirror Therapy Manual by Morkisch & Dohle (2015). During the experiment, the ART system would use these images to display the current exercise to the participant and perform a comparison of that image to the participant's hand movements. Some image processing was applied to the images to ensure they met the requirements expected of the system. The images were then loaded into the designated folders for the system to use.

Once the setup was complete, participants were asked to place their hands under the screen and instructed on what to expect from the system. Then, the first pre-selected condition with their pre-determined hand was initiated. Each condition comprised of three two-minute phases. The participant's task was to perform the hand exercise shown on screen and to try to complete as many exercises as they could within each of the two-minute phases. The instructions given to the participant were that they should move their hand to best match the displayed exercise and maintain their hand position in place. The system would then evaluate and progress the exercises automatically. Before starting their first condition, the participants were told that the instruction and evaluation would be the same for both conditions, but in one condition there would be feedback based on their performance. All exercises were carried out by showing a mirrored display of the hand on the other side of the screen.

After each two-minute phase, participants completed a user experience questionnaire. After completing the first condition (three two-minute phases), they filled out the satisfaction questionnaire. When both conditions had been completed, participants completed the suitability, usability, and final comparison questionnaires. After that, participants were thanked for their time and rewarded with a chocolate bar.

Statistical analysis

Post-phase feedback data from the three phases with feedback was compared to the data from the three phases without feedback. A two-tailed paired-sample t-test was used to compare the performance of participants between the two conditions. A Related-Samples Wilcoxon Signed Rank Test was used to compare the data from the two satisfaction questionnaires completed after each condition. A One-Sample Wilcoxon Signed Rank Test on the medians of the scales with their neutral midpoints was used. Where indicated, values for negatively worded questions were inverted. Analyses for parametric tests were carried out with Microsoft Excel 2013, and non-parametric tests were conducted in SPSS 22.0.0.2. For all analyses, p-values below .05 were considered as statistically significant.

RESULTS AND DISCUSSION

The results of the suitability evaluation questionnaire (SEQ) were statistically significant ($p < .001$) with the averages of all questions above the neutral midpoint "0," showing that overall, participants perceived the system as suitable (Figure 2 left). The ratings of negatively phrased questions Q7–Q10 and Q12 were inverted.

The first seven questions of the SEQ measured enjoyment (Q1), sense of being in the system (Q2), feeling of success (Q3), control (Q4), virtual environment realism (Q5), system information clarity (Q6), and general discomfort (Q7). The high ratings obtained indicated that overall participants enjoyed their experience with the system. However, Q7 had a reasonably low value, indicating that overall participants did not experience a high level of comfort while using the system.

The results obtained for questions Q8–Q10, related to the issues frequently associated with virtual rehabilitation systems, show that participants on average experienced no serious adverse effects such as dizziness (Q8), eye discomfort (Q9) or confusion (Q10). Out of these three questions, Q10 which asked whether a participant felt confused or disorientated had the lowest average value. This was an expected result as many of the participants were initially confused by the mirroring of their hand.

Q11 asked participants whether they believed that the system would be useful for rehabilitation. Although participants may not have knowledge on the field of rehabilitation, this question could still indicate opinions on the suitability of the system. The results were uniformly high and suggested that participants believe the system would be helpful for rehabilitation.

Questions Q12 and Q13 were related to the perceived difficulty. Q12 was the difficulty of the task, which here had a value close to zero. Therefore, the difficulty of the tasks performed by the participants appeared to be neither too difficult nor too easy. As part of the task creation, we would not want to make the task too easy or too difficult. Ideally, the task should feel achievable, engaging, and challenging. Q13 evaluated the perceived difficulty related with the physical interface used in the system and was again positively rated; this was expected as our system only required a participant to move their hands.

Q14 was an open ended question that participants could use to report if there was anything during the experiment that made them feel uncomfortable. Eight participants (28.57%) indicated that they felt uncomfortable in some way when using the system. The written responses included participants feeling uncomfortable sitting so close to the screen, their unused hand feeling sore from holding it still, and specific exercises were causing some soreness.

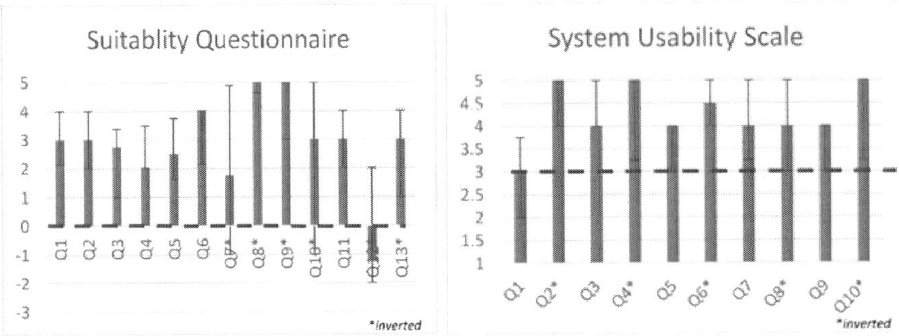

Figure 2. Suitability Evaluation Questionnaire (left), System Usability Scale (right) (Median and IQR bars).

Usability

The results of the usability questionnaire were significantly positive ($p < .001$) with a mean rating of 4, clearly above the neutral midpoint (see Figure 2, right). Note that the ratings of negatively phrased questions (Q2, Q4, Q6, Q8 & Q10) were inverted. The SUS score, calculated using the method proposed by the author of the scale, was 75/100. This was above the pooled average of 68 calculated from more than 3,500 prior applications of the SUS and suggest that participants thought the system has good appropriateness for its purpose, although no strong clinical implications can be made as we conducted the study with healthy participants (18).

Q1 asked how frequently the participant would like to use the system. As the participants were healthy, it was not likely that they would expect to use a rehabilitation system, thus values near the midpoint were not of concern. Participants uniformly rated the complexity of the system (Q2) positively, meaning that the majority of the participants found the system to not be unnecessarily complex. Similarly, participants indicated that the system was not cumbersome (Q8). The system's ease of use (Q3) was also highly rated. The need for a technical person to be able to use the system (Q4) was rated low (i.e., high inverted values), suggesting that overall, participants felt they would be able to use the system on their own. The integration of functions (Q5) was above midpoint, and the inconsistency of the system (Q6) was also positively rated. The learnability of the system was explored in questions Q7 and Q10. Regarding the learnability for other people (Q7), participants indicated that other people would learn to use the system very quickly. For personal learnability (Q10), participants reported similarly high values, suggesting they believed that they did not need to learn a lot before using the system. Participant confidence when using the system (Q9) was also above the neutral midpoint.

Satisfaction (Post-Condition)

The satisfaction questionnaire was completed twice, once after the feedback condition and once after the non-feedback condition. The results (see Figure 3) for both conditions show that participants were very satisfied, with medians clearly above midpoint ($p < .001$). The differences between the two conditions (feedback: *Median*=7.25, *IQR*=1; no-feedback: *Median*=7, *IQR*=2) however did not reach significance ($p = .071$).

Figure 3. Satisfaction (Median with IQR bars) and redline to highlight neutral midpoint.

Performance

Analyses of the performance data did not reveal any significant difference between the feedback and non-feedback conditions, across all three phase. The differences in the amount of performed exercises per phase (no-feedback: *M*=8.1, *SD*=4.69; feedback: *M*=8.11, *SD*=4.77) (p = .38), the accuracy of the execution (no-feedback: *M*=88.46, *SD*=3.83; feedback: *M*=88.02, *SD*=4.98) (p = .35) and the average time required per exercise (no-feedback: *M*=8.58, *SD*=8.12; feedback: *M*=8.50, *SD*=7.18) (p = .10) were not statistically significant.

All participants were able to complete at least one exercise in one of the three phases per session. At 11 instances (6.5%), 6 times in one of the three phases during the first session and 5 times in the second session, a participant finished a phase without successfully completing at least one exercise per phase.

User Experience (post phase)

Levels of user experience were measured after each phase, a total of 6 times, 3 times after phases with feedback and 3 times after phases without feedback. The difference of the overall median of the 6 questions' median was not statistically significant (p = .289) with differences for Q1 (p = .172), Q2 (p = .395), Q3 (p = .930), Q4 (p = .430), Q5 (p = .171) and Q6 (p = .172) all not significant.

Final comparison

The final questionnaire asked participants to directly compare the two conditions on a five-point scale with the feedback condition on the left side of the scale ("−2") and the no-feedback condition on the right side ("+2"). Across all four questions, the data were significantly in favour of ART with feedback (*Median*=−1.5, *IQR*=2) (p = .002). The data for the individual question Q1 (general preference) indicated that participants preferred using the system with feedback (*Median*=−2, *IQR*=1.75) ($p < .001$). The results for Q3 (motivation) also showed that participants felt more motivated with feedback (*Median*=−2, *IQR*=2) ($p = .002$). The ease of use (Q2) was also perceived to be better in the feedback condition (*Median*=−2, *IQR*=2) ($p = .001$). Q4 (ability to concentrate) was also significant (*Median*=0, *IQR*=3), although not as highly as the other questions ($p = .034$).

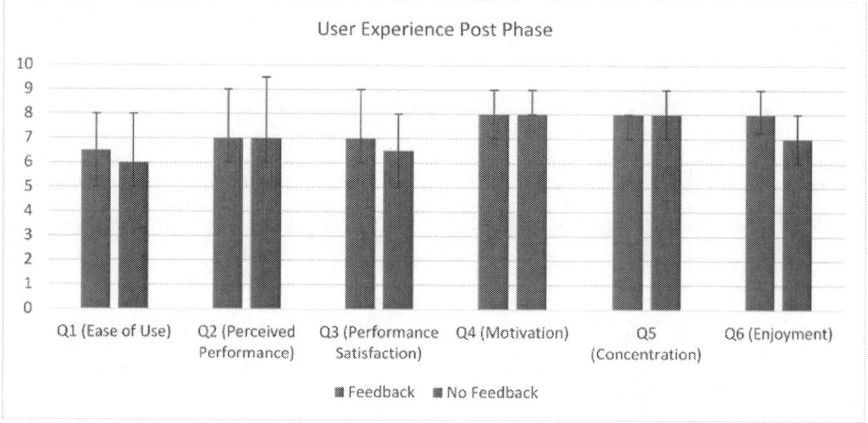

Figure 4. Average user experience across three measurements for each condition (Median and IQR bars).

Conclusion

In this study, we have shown that automated mirror therapy with the ART can be performed with healthy participants and that it is perceived as usable and suitable for rehabilitation by healthy non-clinical participants. We evaluated two versions of the system where we either provided feedback or did not, in addition to giving automated instructions for each exercise. Although we could not find a statistical difference on the satisfaction and general user experience between the conditions with and without feedback, when participants directly compared the two conditions, strong and significant preferences for the feedback conditions were found.

As part of the suitability questionnaire and when queried informally after the experiment session, some participants reported that they experienced discomfort due to their seated position when using the system. This is already an identified area in which further refinement is required, and is not just specific to the version of the ART system presented here. The discomfort specific to this version of ART is the angle in which participants were required to place their hands to align with the on screen image. Some participants found that they had to place themselves at an unnatural position that was sometimes difficult to achieve or hold still for a prolonged time. Possible use with a patient population could be limited due to the identified problems with seating and hand positioning and improving this will be a focus for future development of the ART system.

The number of times a participant was not able to complete an exercise due to various difficulties was low, however to not create any unnecessarily frustration for patient an improvement of this can be the target of future development. For example, the system could switch to a new exercise or lower the required accuracy when a user is not able to accurately perform an exercise for an extended time. With this study, further progress towards an automated system for the provision of mirror therapy was achieved and preparations for clinical evaluations using this system with stroke patients can now be initiated.

ACKNOWLEDGMENTS

The authors thank all participants who took part in this study and Prof Holger Regenbrecht for providing support, feedback and encouragement throughout the period. We also thank Dr Wendy Powell, Dr Vaughan Powell and other experts in the field for their valuable feedback during the developmental phase of the feedback system. This study was part of the dissertation work of Jack Pinches supervised by Dr Simon Hoermann. This study was approved by the University of Otago Ethics Committee.

References

[1] Laver KE, George S, Thomas S, Deutsch JE, Crotty M. Virtual reality for stroke rehabilitation. Cochrane Database Syst Rev 2011;9:CD008349.

[2] Rehabilitation therapy after a stroke [Internet]. Stroke.org, 2015. URL: http://www.stroke.org/we-can-help/stroke-survivors/just-experienced-stroke/rehab.

[3] Hoermann S, Hale L, Winser SJ, Regenbrecht H. Augmented reflection technology for stroke rehabilitation – a clinical feasibility study. In: Sharkey PM, Klinger E, eds. Proceedings 9th International Conference on Disability, Virtual Reality & Associated Technologies. Laval, France, 2012:317–22.

[4] Hoermann S, Ferreira dos Santos L, Morkisch N, Jettkowski K, Sillis M, Cutfield N, et al. Computerized mirror therapy with augmented reflection technology for stroke rehabilitation: A feasibility study in a rehabilitation center. In: Proceedings of the 2015 International Conference on Virtual Rehabilitation. Valencia, Spain: IEEE, 2015.

[5] Mehnert J, Brunetti M, Steinbrink J, Niedeggen M, Dohle C. Effect of a mirror-like illusion on activation in the precuneus assessed with functional near-infrared spectroscopy. J Biomed Opt 2013;18(6):066001.

[6] Michielsen ME, Smits M, Ribbers GM, Stam HJ, Van Der Geest JN, Bussmann JBJ, et al. The neuronal correlates of mirror therapy: An fMRI study on mirror induced visual illusions in patients with stroke. J Neurol Neurosurg Psychiatry 2011; 82(4):393–8.

[7] Ramachandran VS, Rogers-Ramachandran D, Cobb S. Touching the phantom limb. Nature 1995;377(6549):489–90.

[8] Altschuler EL, Wisdom SB, Stone L, Foster C, Galasko D, Llewellyn DME, et al. Rehabilitation of hemiparesis after stroke with a mirror. Lancet 1999;353(9169): 2035–6.

[9] Thieme H, Mehrholz J, Pohl M, Behrens J, Dohle C. Mirror therapy for improving motor function after stroke. Cochrane Database Syst Rev 2012;3:CD008449.

[10] Jettkowski K, Morkisch N, Dohle C. Wie sollte ein Eigentraining für Erwachsene gestaltet sein? Berlin, Germany: Deutsche Gesellschaft für Neurorehabilitation, 2013:396. [German].

[11] Maclean N, Pound P. A critical review of the concept of patient motivation in the literature on physical rehabilitation. Soc Sci Med 2000;50(4):495–506.

[12] Oldfield RC. The assessment and analysis of handedness: The Edinburgh inventory. Neuropsychologia 1971;9(1):97–113.

[13] Regenbrecht H, Botella C, Banos R, Schubert T. Mixed Reality Experience Questionnaire 1.0 [Internet]. Mixed Reality Experience Questionnaire (MREQ) 1.0. 2013. URL: http://www.hci.otago.ac.nz/mreq/MixedRealityExperienceQuestionnaire Web.htm.

[14] Lewis JR. IBM computer usability satisfaction questionnaires: psychometric evaluation and instructions for use. Int J Hum Comput Interact 1995;7(1):57–78.

[15] Gil-Gomez J-A, Manzano-Hernandez P, Albiol-Perez S, Aula-Valero C. SEQ: Suitability Evaluation Questionnaire for Virtual Rehabilitation systems. Application in a virtual rehabilitation system for balance rehabilitation. 2013 7th International Conference on Pervasive Computing Technologies for Healthcare (PervasiveHealth), 2013:335–8.

[16] Brooke J. SUS - A quick and dirty usability scale. Usability Eval Ind 1996;189(194):4–7.

[17] Morkisch N, Dohle C. BeST - Berliner Spiegeltherapieprotokoll: Ein wissenschaftlich evaluiertes Manual zur Durchführung der Spiegeltherapie. Bad Honnef, Germany: Hippocampus Verlag, 2015.

[18] Brooke J. SUS: A retrospective. J Usability Stud 2013;8(2):29–40.

In: Rehabilitation
Editors: Wendy Powell et al.
ISBN: 978-1-53612-080-6

Chapter 6

FACE TO FACE: AN INTERACTIVE FACIAL EXERCISE SYSTEM FOR STROKE PATIENTS WITH FACIAL WEAKNESS

Philip Breedon*[1,*]*, PhD, BSc (Hons), MBCS, FRSA, CEng, CITP, Pip Logan*[2]*, PhD, MPhil, BSc, David Pearce*[3]*, PhD, MSc, MEng (Oxon), CPA, EPA, Judi Edmans*[2]*, PhD, MPhil, Dip COT, Ben Childs*[4]*, MSc, BA and Rebecca O'Brien*[2]*, PGDip, MA, BA (Hons), MRCSLT

[1]Design for Health and Wellbeing Research Group, Nottingham Trent University, Nottingham, United Kingdom
[2]Faculty of Medicine and Health Sciences, Queens Medical Centre, University of Nottingham, Nottingham, United Kingdom
[3]Barker Brettell LLP, Birmingham, United Kingdom
[4]Maddison Product Design Ltd, Fittleworth, United Kingdom

---

[*] Correspondence: Professor Philip Breedon, PhD, BSc (Hons), MBCS, FRSA, CEng, CITP, Professor of Smart Technologies, Design for Health and Wellbeing Research Group, Nottingham Trent University, 50 Shakespeare St, Nottingham NG1 4FQ, United Kingdom. Email: philip.breedon@ntu.ac.uk.

Each year 152,000 people in the United Kingdom have a stroke. Almost all have an initial facial weakness. Many resolve in the first few days but it is estimated that 26,000 people experience some kind of long-term paralysis in their face. A survey of 107 United Kingdom based clinicians found that routine treatment of facial weakness was provision of exercises with a written instruction sheet. A multidisciplinary team, which includes patients, researchers and therapists have produced a working prototype system to improve facial weakness. It is called Face to Face and includes a Kinect sensor, a small form PC and a monitor. Patients follow exercises given by a therapist on the screen; the system records and simultaneously gives feedback, with a facial recognition algorithm providing tracking data for each captured frame of the user's face. Results from our small clinical trial indicate that the system is more successful at getting patients to complete their exercises than using a mirror, patients liked it, and they said it had helped improve their facial symmetry. Therapists said Facc to Facc encouraged patients to exercise daily, they liked the fact that it could be individually programmed and could record how much the patient had exercised. Based on the initial project work and positive outcomes Face to Face aims to help patients practice their facial muscle exercises to speed their recovery, providing direct benefits in terms of costs and time, and offering patients significant improvements.

INTRODUCTION

The overall aim of the project was to test an effective, engaging and affordable interactive facial exercise system for use with people with facial weakness following stroke. This is to meet patient and clinical needs and lead to measurable improvements in clinical outcomes (1-3).

Face to Face is a computer based system that enhances and automates the therapy provided by Speech and Language Therapists (SLTs). The system is initially aimed at stroke survivors suffering from facial paralysis, particularly with stroke patients suffering from swallowing and speech problems. The project development team also propose that the system may become a ‘platform’ system and be adapted and used more widely for a number of conditions and associated facial weakness.

A partnership between Nottingham Trent University, Nottingham CityCare Partnership, University of Nottingham, an industrial partner and service users within the UK have produced a system for use in the home, which uses the Microsoft Kinect games interface and a PC monitor to develop an interactive system to assist in the rehabilitation of patients with facial weakness. The aim is that patients will use this system to complete exercise programmes by copying on-screen exercises, and as they do this the system will monitor and *measure* the patient's face. Members of the University of Nottingham Stroke Research Partnership Group confirm the need for facial paralysis rehabilitation; currently there is a lack of appropriate and affordable alternatives in the market.

The system recognises facial expressions by tracking movement across the face and applying the recognised motion onto an onscreen representation of the user. This tool recognises differences between an undesirable one sided (unilateral) movement and a desired symmetrical movement across both sides of the face. This information is then conveyed via the monitor using the form of a graphical representation of the patients face. Using the representation as both a visual and auditory communicator, the system takes the patient through a series of exercises and indicates the degree of success with the exercise programme. An international patent application for the system was filed in 2015 (4).

Patient benefit

A key aspect of the system is the ability to visualise the improvements that the patient is making from repeated exercises. The system is simple to set up, with no need to attach any systems or markers to the face. The user interface permits small bursts of exercises to be performed throughout the day, rather than undertaking one long and tiring session. The overall aim of the initial project study was to test an effective, engaging and affordable interactive facial exercise system for use with people with facial weakness following stroke. This is to meet patient and clinical needs and lead to measurable improvements in clinical outcomes. The system has the potential to be of benefit to patients by: improving fidelity in rehabilitative exercises prescribed for facial weakness; providing immediate feedback to patients on their progress; improving patient's facial weakness, including carers in the rehabilitation process (a Stroke Association recommendation); assisting patients in meeting the recommended target of 45 minutes daily therapy and reducing the need for patients to visit hospital for rehabilitation.

Clinical need

Approximately 16% of people suffering stroke have long lasting facial weakness (5). A combination of physiotherapy, occupational therapy and speech therapy has been proven to be clinically effective in the treatment of those who have suffered facial weakness following a Stroke. However, whereas the National Clinical Guideline for Stroke (6) indicates that patients should receive 45 minutes of therapeutic treatment daily, the majority of patients receive far less than this. The Royal College of Physicians National Sentinel Stroke Clinical Audit (7) states that only 33% of patients receive 45 minutes or more physiotherapy daily and only 18% of patients receive 45 minutes or more speech and language therapy daily.

It is clear from previous studies, and from involvement with partners at Nottingham University Hospital and the Stroke Association, that there are currently insufficient resources within the NHS to provide the necessary level of therapeutic care post Stroke. The most common rehabilitative exercises prescribed to facial weakness sufferers are either practising motions in front of a mirror or using an instructional DVD. These methods cannot be considered as engaging, due to their lack of feedback and quantifiable progression. Less commonly available is an electrical muscle stimulator designed for facial uses. This machine is made by the NHS electronics departments, and is in short supply, with recipients tending to get a maximum of six weeks to use the system before it is given to the next patient. The machine electrically stimulates the affected muscles to the point that they get exercise through contraction. It is reported to work well in the short term, but owing to short supply and the high price of working machines, along with a lot of training required on the part of the user, it is not currently considered a sustainable solution.

Initial system concepts

Initial system design concepts were based on the utilisation of the patient's own TV with a 'plug and play' 3D system attached. Over a development period of 18 months the preferred options were discussed and agreed with the patient and public involvement group (PPI), resulting in a PPI informed user interface and physical system design based on the Kinect sensor as shown in Figure 1.

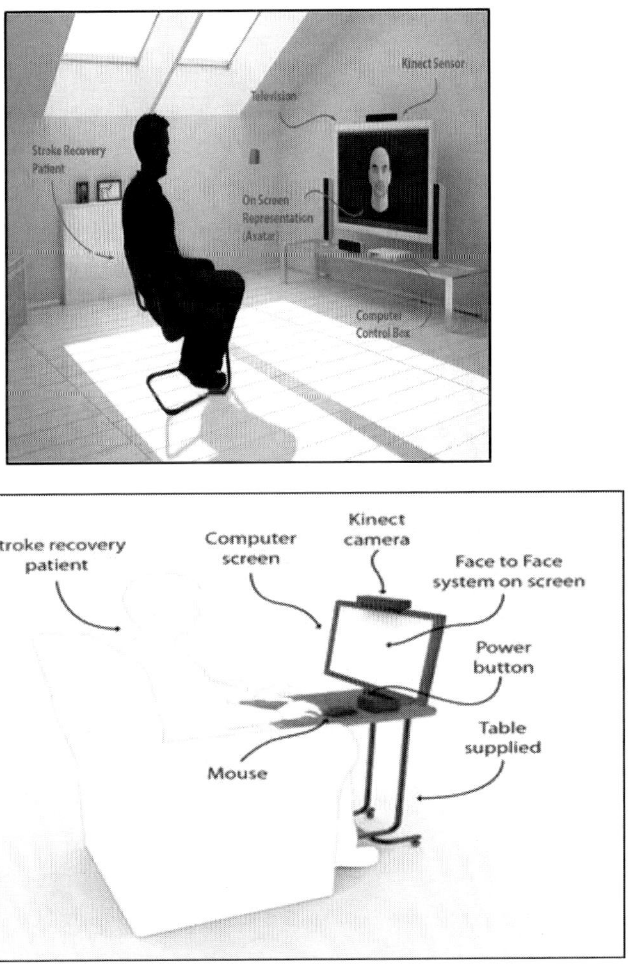

Figure 1. Initial concept (inset) and PPI informed system design.

The system that has been developed as a result of this project recognises facial expressions by tracking movement across the face and applying the recognised motion onto an onscreen representation of the user. How the user performs a series of facial exercises is assessed by the system and scored according to how well the user can do each of a defined set of expressions. The therapist is provided with a record of exercises as they were performed. New movements can be introduced automatically, with incrementally achievable goals throughout the week. The system will enable shorter consultations through the presentation of quantified improvement and empower the carer and the stroke survivors to take on some of the role of supervising the performance of the exercises.

It is proposed that the 'home rehabilitation' solution would help offset some of the problems associated with transfer from hospital to home care. The "Moving On" report (8) states that 48% of Stroke survivors believed that community and home-based therapy helped them become less long term reliant on carers.

System overview

Game based technology platforms are now widely used for physical rehabilitation of patients, recognised as a potential motivational tool for rehabilitation. New opportunities in rehabilitation have clearly arisen with emerging technologies of computer games and novel input sensors including 3D cameras. Hossein and Khademi (9) provided a review on the technical and clinical impact of the Kinect on physical therapy and rehabilitation. Omelina et al. (10) examined serious games for physical rehabilitation and Webster and Ozkan (11) provided a detailed review of elderly care and stroke rehabilitation systems utilising the Kinect. As 3D facial image processing for this research project provides clear additional pose mapping functionality, the benefits of processing depth information when compared to 2D vision systems was explored by González-Ortega et al. (12) in relation to Kinect based systems for cognitive rehabilitation exercise monitoring.

Currently the system has been developed utilising pre-existing facial recognition software known as Faceshift (available from www.faceshift.com and now owned by Apple). Image data is acquired from the Kinect and, when a face is detected, a model is generated of the user's face. A profile can be stored for each user by capturing a pre-set series of expression, with an increased level of accuracy obtained by placing markers on a scanned face. This setup routine may be performed typically by a speech and language therapist (SLT), but should only need to be carried out once, following which the user can operate the system independently.

OUR STUDY

A short review on image processing was conducted by Samsudin and Sundaraj (13) for facial paralysis and facial rehabilitation, identifying image processing as being widely utilised but with very limited applications in relation to facial rehabilitation. Further Xiaozheng and Gao (14) provided a critical review of face recognition techniques and the clear challenges particularly in relation to pose invariant face recognition, whilst Wang et al. (15) examined real time movement linked to an evaluation of skeletal pose tracking using the Microsoft Kinect first and second generation hardware.

Clearly various complications in computer vision require an assessment of pose objects in real-time with numerous reliable solutions available for pose estimation utilising feature-based 3D tracking. However difficulties can arise based on the need for fast and robust detection of known objects in view, for example the Kinect sensors used for this project were notably affected by ambient lighting conditions.

For the Face to Face system, once the facial recognition software is set up to track a user's face the facial recognition algorithm provides tracking data for each captured frame of a user's face. The tracking data relates to a number of facial gestures, together with a value associated with each gesture. In Faceshift, 48 channels of raw tracking data are provided per frame, each of which is associated with a number ranging between 0 and 1. The numbers, or scores, represent the strength of deformation on the 48 predefined gestural channels. For example, the gestural channel 'BrowsD_L' measures lowering of the left eyebrow, and 'LipsStretch_L' measures sideways movement of the left corner of the mouth. These numbers do not represent physical units, but are relative scores defined by upper and lower limits of each facial gesture. These scores are then used to analyse how well the user is performing a particular facial expression.

The speech and language therapist (SLT) defines a number of facial expressions, the facial expressions being specific to a user's rehabilitation programme. These facial expressions can each be defined as a combination of facial gestures that can be captured by the facial tracking algorithm, with each facial gesture having an associated target score. The overall aim of an exercise programme setup for a user is to encourage the user to perform the facial expressions and have these analysed and scored by the computer, using the facial recognition algorithm. To do this, a measure of how well the user is performing a particular facial expression needs to be defined. The mathematical space of tracking variables obtained from the facial recognition algorithm is mapped into a target space of facial gestures (or 'poses') for a particular facial expression. For each pose a measure termed a 'pose match strength' may be defined, for example as another number ranging between 0 and 1.

Pose match strength can be computed from the source tracking channels by defining a subset of the source channels as 'pose channels' that influence the pose match strength value for the facial expression being assessed. Source channels that are not included in a particular pose definition can either be ignored or treated as 'wildcards' for the match, for which any value will match. These represent channels that are irrelevant to the facial expression being exercised. As an example, mouth poses typically would not depend on eyebrow positions, resulting in the values for any eyebrow-related channels being discounted in an assessment of a mouth-related pose. Included pose channels may each define a target value or score for the pose, typically over the input range of between 0 and 1). This score is used to calculate an individual channel match value (again between 0 and 1). The range of input source channel values, i.e., from a minimum to a target value, is linearly mapped to an output pose channel match of 0 to 1. Beyond the target value the output pose channel match is capped at 1.

Figure 2 shows a pose tracking value over time, as defined by 14 successive samples, with a pose match peak of 0.8 and a peak value defined at 0.7 based on the development of the pose tracking value. During each 'out of pose' phase (while the system is looking for an 'in pose' event), whenever the instantaneous tracking value reaches a new highest value this 'pose match peak' value is recorded, and the time is recorded. A moving average is then maintained over the 'time since last peak', which will start at the peak and gradually decline as the instantaneous match strength diminishes.

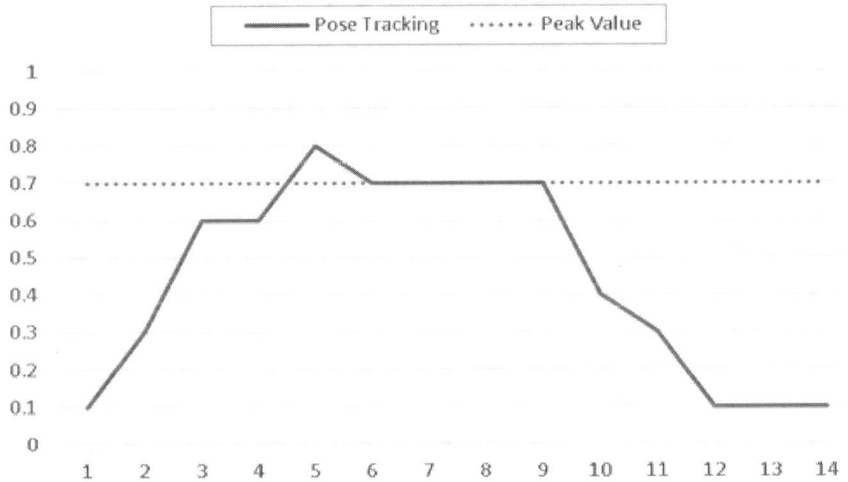

Figure 2. Pose tracking over time (samples 1 to 14).

Once a predefined time threshold is reached (which may, for example be around 0.5 seconds, and typically less than one second) without a new peak value being observed, an enter pose event is triggered and the current moving average is stored as a match value for the current 'active' pose. Conversely if a new instantaneous peak value is reached before the time threshold is reached, a new peak value is recorded, the timer is reset, and a new moving average measurement begins. This can happen several times before reaching a stable peak, particularly if the signal is noisy and/or the peak value is relatively low. The partially unsuccessful short-duration peaks before the final successful peak are analogous to 'false horizons' that are due to noise in the signal, whereas the moving average represents an adaptive threshold which continually adjusts to varying user ability and tracking response.

Each pose channel included in the pose definition may be marked as either a goal or a constraint. The output pose match strength is a relative score that can be calculated as the maximum of the set of all computed goal pose channel match values, limited by the minimum of the set of all constraint pose channel match values. This is similar to goal channels acting as logical 'OR' and constraint channels acting as logical 'AND'. The score for each facial gesture may be defined as a ratio of a score for the facial gesture provided by the facial recognition algorithm to the target score for the facial gesture. The score may range between 0 and 1, and be limited to 1 if the ratio exceeds 1.

FINDINGS

Each of the exercise types relies on a predefined series of steps, these steps are illustrated in Figure 3. The process begins with an on-screen instruction phase with an acknowledgement when the number of repetitions has been completed. In between these two phases, the exercise involves looking for a particular target pose at any given time, which may even apply in the case of speed exercises which involve alternating between two poses. When an exercise target pose begins, the state is initially 'out of pose' and the system waits for the user to enter the pose. Once in pose, the system waits for the pose match strength to drop below a predetermined threshold value.

The events of entering and exiting a current target pose can trigger different responses depending on the exercise type. For example, speed exercises may switch to an alternate pose on exiting a first pose, whereas range exercises tend to set an 'anti-pose' during a relax phase which the user must enter (for example open mouth, followed by closed mouth) before returning to the original target pose for the next repetition (open mouth).

Once the user is in pose the user is instructed to hold for a set period, and once the set period elapses the process can then repeat if required or complete. The series of steps involved in performing an exercise transforms a continuous range of pose match strengths into a series of discrete states and state change events. The user interface indicates the number of repetitions, which then triggers the next instructional video (“open your mouth...” / “...and relax”).

A particular problem, however, arises when considering how to determine when a particular pose has been achieved, i.e., when the state should change from 'out of pose' to 'in pose'. This determination can be made because of a continuous assessment of the score for a facial expression that is the subject of the exercise.

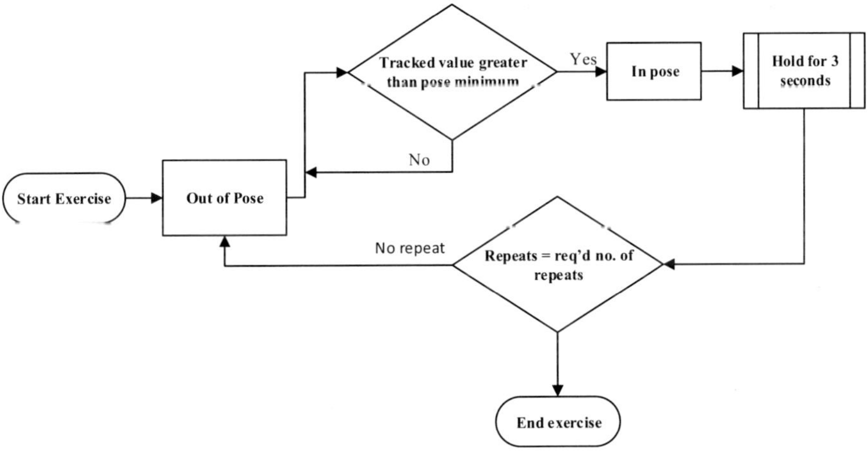

Figure 3. Exercise steps.

Pose example

The ‘ee’ pose may be defined by MouthSmile_L (left) and MouthSmile_R (right) as goal channels, each with a target value of 0.8, defining JawOpen as an inverted constraint channel with a target value of 0.5. The following two conditions then result:

Condition 1:
MouthSmile_L = 0.2 - goal match 0.2/0.8 = 0.25
MouthSmile_R = 0.6 - goal match 0.6/0.8 = 0.75
JawOpen = 0.3 - inverted constraint match = 1
(less than target 0.5, inverted, capped to 1)
Pose match strength = min (max (goal),
min (constraint)) = min (0.75, 1) = 0.75

Condition 2:
MouthSmile_L = 0.2 goal match 0.2/0.8 = 0.25
MouthSmile_R = 0.6 - goal match 0.6/0.8 = 0.75
JawOpen = 0.8 inverted constraint match = (1 - 0.8) /
(1 - 0.5) = 0.2/0.5 = 0.40
Pose match strength = min (max (goal),
min (constraint)) = min (0.75, 0.40) = 0.40

This example could be interpreted as: an 'ee' pose requiring MouthSmile Left OR Right, AND jaw mostly closed. In the second scenario, the pose match strength is reduced to 0.4 because the jaw constraint is infringed, limiting the overall output value. In more general terms, a relative score for each identified facial gesture in a facial expression is calculated as a ratio of the score for each identified facial gesture to the corresponding target score for the facial gesture. The score for the facial expression can be calculated based on a maximum relative score for the facial gestures defining the facial expression. Other combinations of goals and constraints can also be determined, depending on the particular facial expression to be exercised and whether any particular constraints need to be considered. For example, a facial exercise regime may be made up from a set of nine different poses. These may be combined using 9 range exercises with 9 strength exercises and with 3 poses used in pairs in 'fast' and 'slow' versions to make up 6 speed exercises (AB, AC, BC x fast/slow), making a total of 24 exercises to be performed in the exercise regime. A therapist can then make a patient assessment, and simply enable or disable each exercise from this palette of 24 exercises to quickly construct a tailored exercise regime for that user. A screenshot pose is shown in Figure 4 and the patient progress screen in Figure 5.

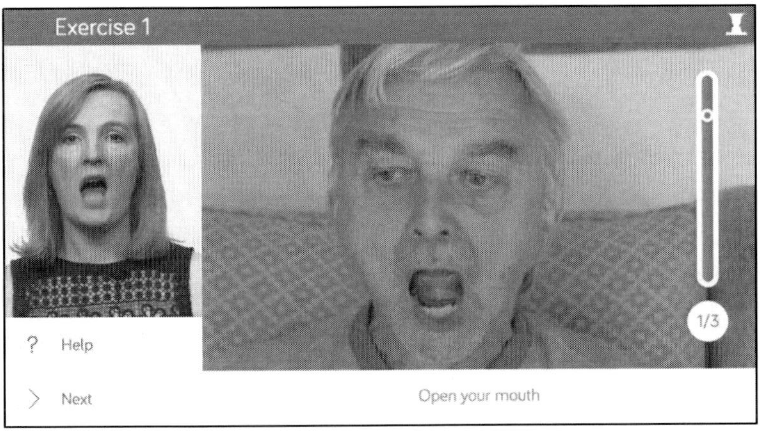

Figure 4. Exercise pose screenshot with a graphical indication of the user's score (right) and exercise number (bottom right) overlaid on a picture of the user next to an image showing the pose to be performed. The pose indicated by a speech and language therapist (left).

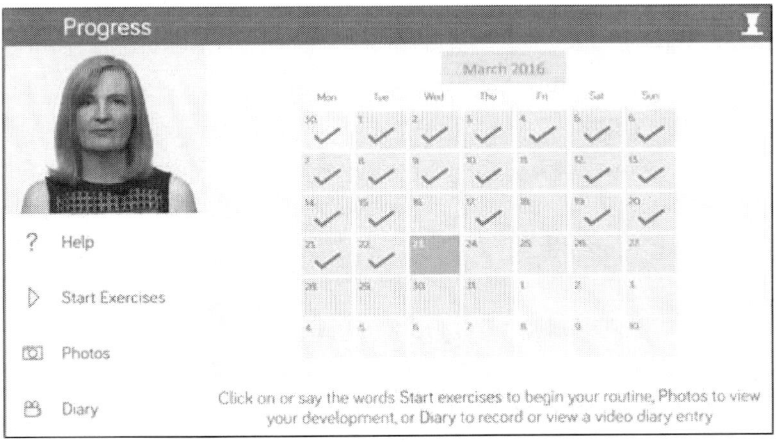

Figure 5. System diary and progress screen.

Discussion

Participants found the Face to Face system to be a user-friendly rehabilitation tool for facial weakness after stroke, usage indicated that all participants were motivated to use the system (16). All participants made a slight improvement from baseline assessment and the therapist observed that: there was possible synkinesis in one participant and there was no deterioration or worsening of this following use of Face to Face system; one participant's ability to speak improved which increased confidence; one participant's natural smile became almost symmetrical and reduced drooling and reduced numbness was reported by one participant, leading to positive comments.

The speech and language therapist (SLT) and all participants noted functional changes and detected clinical changes in the level of facial weakness subjectively. The SLT assessed the level of facial weakness using the Sunnybrook facial grading system (17, 18) and prescribed a treatment plan of facial exercises from the Face to Face programme.

Currently development is focused on transforming tracking data received from the facial recognition algorithm into pose match strengths against a combination of facial gestures, the system enables a straightforward means of constructing and performing an exercise regime. In addition, development of a complex and informative web-based interface for clinical evaluation of patient's use and performance against rehabilitation regimes has been created. This will provide real-time adherence data during rehabilitation and allow a personalised exercise plan to be adjusted remotely, at any time, depending on patient's actual exercise patterns and improvements.

Looking forward, there is a growing number of technologies coming to market that will benefit and enhance this product. Of particular interest is the *new* 3D camera technology launched by Intel. These 3D cameras use the same principles as the Kinect camera but are designed to be integrated into phones, tablets and laptops. Another important feature of the Intel cameras is that they have been specially designed to focus on facial recognition and tracking, this will provide an accurate and reliable facial tracking system for us to use. In contrast the Kinect system is designed for full body tracking, although the system can be used to track facial expressions it is not its primary function and therefore limits the effectiveness of the product and requires a payment for third party software licences.

In current practice, SLTs priorities are in assessing and planning the patient's therapy, and non-professional assistant practitioners (APs) are used on a day-to-day basis with the patient to monitor adherence to the program and assist the patient. We propose to extend the stored usage database to include a record of planned usage regimes for each patient, and to provide a visual comparison of actual usage against the planned regime in the web interface. This approach would allow an AP to interpret the live usage data in the web interface, identifying overuse or underuse of exercises without needing to involve an SLT in the first instance. The web-based interface would still be accessible to SLTs who could perform any further analysis they felt necessary, but they would now also be able to remotely adjust the exercise regime while the device was still in the patient's home. Further development of the product is required and to address other market opportunities, including: improving the user interface to address shortcomings identified in trials and research; improving the compactness and portability of the physical embodiment; strengthening the robustness and functionality of the system (for example in low light conditions); reducing unit cost and finally allowing for a wider range of exercises, implying a more complex interface requirement to allow SLTs to set up systems for patients.

It is anticipated that this additional functionality would reduce the ongoing costs of deploying the final system within everyday healthcare practice, by reducing the required time from the SLT.

ACKNOWLEDGMENTS

The authors also gratefully acknowledge the invaluable support and contributions to the project from: Ossie Newell MBE, The stroke service (PPI) group, Adam Russell and Paul Watts (both previously based at

Nottingham Trent University, UK), Patrick Hall at Maddison and Claire Wragg at NTU. The Face to Face project was funded by the NIHR Invention for Innovation Programme (i4i). The views expressed are those of the authors and not necessarily those of the NHS, the NIHR or the Department of Health.

REFERENCES

[1] Breedon P. Face to Face: An interactive facial exercise system for stroke patients with facial, talking technology. Current trends in speech and language therapy. London: Association Speech Language Therapists Independent Practice (ASLTIP), 2015.

[2] Breedon P, Russell A, Logan P, Newell, O, O'Brien B., Edmans J, et al. First for stroke: Using the Microsoft' Kinect' as a facial paralysis stroke rehabilitation tool. Int J Integr Care 2014;14:8. Doi.org/10.5334/ijic.1760.

[3] O'Brien R. Facial weakness after stroke. Harrogate, UK: UK Stroke Forum, 2014.

[4] PCT/GB2015/053623. International patent application, 2016.

[5] Svensson BH, Christiansen LS, Jepsen E. Treatment of central facial nerve paralysis with electromyography biofeedback and taping of cheek. A controlled clinical trial. Ugeskrift Laeger 1992;154(50):3593-6 [Danish].

[6] Intercollegiate Stroke Working Party. National Clinical Guidelines for Stroke: Fourth edition. London: Royal College Physicians, 2012. URL: https://www.rcplondon.ac.uk/guidelines-policy/stroke-guidelines.

[7] National Sentinel Stroke Audit, (1998 – 2010). URL: https://www.rcplondon.ac.uk/projects/national-sentinel-stroke-audit-nssa.

[8] Chartered Society of Physiotherapy and Stroke Association. Moving on: A vision for community based after stroke in England. London: Stroke Association, 2010.

[9] Hossein HM, Khademi M. A review on technical and clinical impact of Microsoft Kinect on physical therapy and rehabilitation. J Med Engineering 2014;2014:846514. Doi.org/10.1155/2014/846514.

[10] Omelina L, Jansen B, Bonnechere B, Van Sint Jan S, Cornelis J. Serious games for physical rehabilitation: designing highly configurable and adaptable games. Proceedings of the 9th International Conference on Disability, Virtual Reality and Associated Technologies, Reading, Berkshire, United Kingdom, 2012.

[11] Webster D, Ozkan C. Systematic review of Kinect applications in elderly care and stroke rehabilitation. J Neuroengineering Rehabil 2014;11(1):1.

[12] González-Ortega D, Díaz-Pernas FJ, Martínez-Zarzuela M, Antón-Rodríguez M. A Kinect-based system for cognitive rehabilitation exercises monitoring. Comput Methods Programs Biomed 2014;113(2):620-31.

[13] Samsudin WSW, Sundaraj K. Image processing on facial paralysis for facial rehabilitation system: A review. Control System, Computing and Engineering (ICCSCE), IEEE, 2012.

[14] Zhang X, Gao Y. Face recognition across pose: A review. Pattern Recogn 2009;42(11):2876-96.

[15] Wang Q, Kurillo G, Ofli F, Bajcsy R. Evaluation of pose tracking accuracy in the first and second generations of Microsoft Kinect. Healthcare Informatics (ICHI), International Conference. IEEE, 2015.

[16] Edmans J, Breedon P, Childs B, Hall P, Newell O, O'Brien B, et al. Face to Face: An exploratory trial of a facial rehabilitation tool for facial weakness after stroke. Neurol Pract Newsletter 2016;49:40-7.

[17] Hu WL, Ross B, Nedzelski J. Reliability of the Sunnybrook Facial Grading System by novice users. J Otolaryngol 2001;30:208–11.

[18] Ross BG, Fradet G, Nedzelski JM. Development of a sensitive clinical facial grading system. Otolaryngol Head Neck Surg 1996;114(3):380-6.

In: Rehabilitation
Editors: Wendy Powell et al.
ISBN: 978-1-53612-080-6

Chapter 7

AUGMENTED FEEDBACK APPROACH TO DOUBLE-LEG SQUAT TRAINING FOR PATIENTS WITH KNEE OSTEOARTHRITIS: A PRELIMINARY STUDY

Mohammad Al-Amri[1,*], PhD, Jennifer L Davies[1], PhD, Paul Adamson[1,2], MSc, Kate Button[1,2,3], PhD, Paulien E Roos[1,4], PhD and Robert van Deursen[1,3], PhD

[1]School of Healthcare Sciences, Cardiff University, Heath, Cardiff, United Kingdom,
[2]Physiotherapy Department, Cardiff and Vale UHB, Heath, Cardiff, United kingdom,
[3]Arthritis Research UK Biomechanics and Bioengineering Centre, Cardiff University, Cardiff, United Kingdom and
[4]CFD Research Corporation, Huntsville, Alabama, US

[*]Correspondence: Mohammad Al-Amri, PhD, Research Associate, School of Healthcare Studies, Heath Park, Cardiff University, Cardiff CF14 4XN, United Kingdom. Email: Al-amriM@cardiff.ac.uk.

In this chapter we explore the effects of two types of augmented feedback on the strategy used by healthy participants and patients with knee osteoarthritis (OA) to perform a double-leg squat. Seven patients with knee OA and seven healthy participants performed three sets of eight double-leg squats: one without feedback, one with real-time kinematic feedback and one with real-time kinetic feedback. Kinematic and kinetic outcome measures (peak knee flexion angle, peak knee extensor moment, and symmetry of the support knee moment between the injured and non-injured knees) demonstrate the potential influence of real-time kinetic feedback on the motor strategy used to perform a double-leg squat in both groups. This feedback could be used to develop more efficient and effective motor strategies for squatting in patients with knee OA and further evaluation is warranted.

INTRODUCTION

Knee osteoarthritis (OA) is the most common heterogeneous joint disease. Musculoskeletal pain associated with knee OA can hamper the performance of daily living activities and influence wellbeing (1, 2). Physical performance of daily living activities is an important indicator of the impact of knee OA and resulting pain on individuals' quality of life (2-4). There are currently no known treatments to slow the progression of OA; however, physiotherapy is one approach used to improve management of the condition (5-8).

Neuromuscular physiotherapy typically includes physical exercise programmes focusing on strengthening, improving and maintaining aptitude for controlling and regulating postural stability, balance, and muscular strength (9), and can improve mobility and strength in patients with knee OA. The exercise programmes require interaction between neural systems and musculoskeletal systems to generate forces to accomplish body movements (10, 11).

Innovative physiotherapy tools are needed to improve physical exercise adherence in individuals with OA and should focus on enhancing self-efficacy and enjoyment. Interventions that consider self-efficacy, maintaining motivation and engagement may successfully achieve functional improvements in patients with OA, who often engage and adhere less in physical activity than non-diseased populations (12, 13). A possible innovative approach to guide physical exercise performance through feedback and increase patients' engagement is the inclusion of virtual reality into physical exercises (14-16). Virtual reality is a technology that allows a user to interact with a computer-simulated environment, be it real or imagined (17). Using this technology, we have explored the feasibility of providing in-house-developed real-time targeted feedback of kinetic performance during squatting in game context (18).

Considering the importance of implementing a real-time feedback system in a clinical setting, we have developed our targeted feedback application in conjunction with a clinical team. The application is being developed to use simple kinetic data that can be obtained from affordable and simple equipment that is marketed for entertainment purposes, such as the commercial Nintendo Wii balance board (19, 20). We are developing the application for the double-leg squat, as this is commonly used in clinical settings to assess and strengthen muscles around the knee (21).

As part of the development process, we are conducting research to understand the influence of two types of feedback (kinematic and kinetic) on the biomechanics of the double-legged squat. The kinematic feedback comprises a stick figure, which represents the subject, being presented on a screen in front of the subject, enabling the subject to view their movement. The kinetic feedback is presented in the context of a game, and requires subjects to focus on the effects of their movements by adjusting the net centre of pressure (COPnet) under their feet to match a target provided on the screen in front of them. The overall aim of this work is to make a preliminary assessment of the effects of an in-house-developed real-time targeted feedback application on the kinetics of a double-leg squat in patients with knee OA. The long-term aim of this research is to determine whether an augmented, real-time, targeted biofeedback approach can aid patients with knee OA by facilitating an effective motor learning strategy and improving self-efficacy.

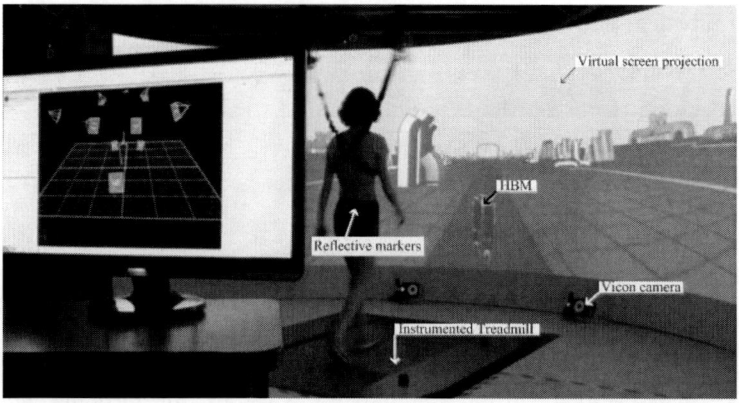

Figure 1. Cardiff Gait Real-time Analysis Interactive Lab.

OUR STUDY

The experimental set up compromised the Cardiff Gait Real-time Analysis Interactive Lab system (see Figure 1, GRAIL, Motek Medical, Amsterdam, The Netherlands), which consists of an instrumented split-belt treadmill, a 12-camera Vicon MX optical infrared tracking system (Oxford Metrics, Oxford, UK) and synchronised 3D environments that were developed using Google Sketchup (version 8.0, Google, USA). D-Flow software (version 3.20.1, Motek Medical, the Netherlands) was used in the development of the feedback applications and their implementation on the GRAIL system.

Participant recruitment

The South East Wales Local Research Ethics Committee approved this research. Inclusion criteria for knee OA patients were: a consultant's diagnosis of knee OA both clinically and radiographically, aged between 18 and 75 years, no previous musculoskeletal surgery in the past 12 months and no other pathologies that affect their movements, no evidence of photosensitive epilepsy, and able to follow simple instructions. Inclusion criteria for healthy participants were: aged between 18 and 75 years and no conditions that affect their movement. Patients were recruited from patients attending physiotherapy clinics.

Procedure

The investigation was carried out in the Research Centre for Clinical Kinesiology at Cardiff University. On arrival, participants were oriented to the laboratory and the study procedures, and consented to the study protocol if they were happy to participate. Demographic, anthropometric (including height and mass) and relevant clinical information (including condition history and any other related medical conditions that may affect knee OA) were then obtained via questionnaire and interview. Patients with knee OA completed the Oxford Knee Score, a validated, knee-specific instrument designed to gather opinion about their knee and associated problems, and all participants completed the Tegner Activity Scale form (22), a validated measure of activity level. Forty-seven reflective markers were placed on anatomical landmarks using the Motek Human Body Model full-body marker set (Motek Medical, the Netherlands).

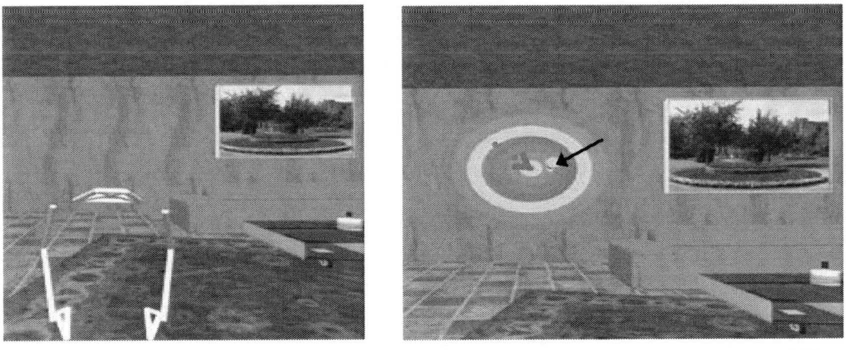

(A) (B)

Figure 2. A screenshot of the virtual room during the kinematic feedback condition (A) and the kinetic feedback condition (B). In B the blue arrow refers to the target position (where the symmetry support moment is 100%) and the black arrow refers to the virtual object that driven by the actual symmetry support moment.

Each participant performed eight continuous double-leg squats at their comfortable speed and to a comfortable depth under three conditions whilst they were standing on a stationary instrumented treadmill. The first condition was without feedback, the second condition was with kinematic feedback (a real-time stick-figure of the lower limbs presented in a virtual living room; see Figure 2A), and the third condition was with kinetic feedback (net centre of pressure [COPnet] presented as a virtual object on a virtual arrow mat; see Figure 2B). For the kinetic feedback condition, participants were instructed to keep the virtual object as close as possible to the centre of the virtual arrow mat. COP data were obtained through force plates embedded within the stationary treadmill (Forcelink, Culemborg, the Netherlands) and COPnet was calculated in the anterior/posterior (A/P) and medial/lateral (M/L) directions within Motek D-Flow software (version 3.20.1) using equation (1) (23). Initial COPnet was computed whilst participants were standing with a body weight evenly distributed across the left and right feet, and was used to calibrate the virtual object.

$$COPnet = COP_l \frac{R_l}{R_l+R_r} + COP_r \frac{R_r}{R_l+R_r} \tag{1}$$

where $COPnet$: net of centre of pressure; COP_l: left centre of pressure; COP_r: right centre of pressure; R_l: left vertical reaction force; and R_r: right vertical reaction force.

Data analysis and processing

Joint and segment angles and moments were calculated using the Motek Human Body Model within D-Flow software (version 3.20.1). The following outcome measures were calculated using Matlab R2015b (Mathworks Inc. USA): peak knee flexion angle, peak knee extensor moment, symmetry of the support knee moment between the injured and non-injured knees (knee OA patients) or between the dominant and non-dominant knees (healthy participants), and total symmetry of the support moment between injured/dominant and non-injured/non-dominant legs. The symmetry support moment (%SYSM) was calculated using equation (2) (24).

$$\%SYSM = \frac{2*\text{Left Moment}}{\text{Left Moment}+\text{Right Moment}} * 100 \quad (2)$$

As this is an exploratory study with a small sample size we did not undertake any statistical tests within or between groups. Descriptive analysis of all outcome measures and demographic data was performed using Microsoft Excel 2013 (Microsoft, USA).

FINDINGS

Seven knee OA patients (gender: four males, three females, height: 171.5 ± 7.2 cm, mass: 87.5 ± 17.2 kg, age: 52.1 ± 10.6 years) were compared to seven healthy volunteers (gender: two males, five females, height: 169.4 ± 8.3 cm, mass: 73.1 ± 15.3 kg, age: 45.0 ± 12.4 years). Details of the participants are summarised in Table 1.

Table 1. Participant characteristics. Data are means ± standard deviation. OA, osteoarthritis; CONT, healthy control participants; OKS, Oxford Knee Score; Tegner, Tegner Activity Scale; BMI, body mass index

	Age (years)	Height (cm)	Mass (kg)	BMI	OKS	Tegner
Knee OA	52.1 ± 10.6	171.5 ± 7.2	87.5 ± 17.2	29.6 ± 3.8	35 ± 5.1	3.7 ± 2.3
CONT	45 ± 12.4	169.4 ± 8.3	73.1 ± 15.3	25.4 ± 4.1	N/A	6.6 ± 1.4

Knee flexion angle

Figure 3 shows the average peak knee flexion angle for each knee across conditions and groups. The difference between groups in the absence of feedback, with kinematic feedback (stick figure) and with kinetic feedback

(COPnet target) was 14o, 15o and 10o, respectively. The greatest variability occurred in the kinetic feedback condition, and was at least 2o higher compared to the first and second conditions across groups. The difference in average peak knee flexion angle between the injured/non-dominant leg and healthy/dominant leg was less than 2o in all conditions.

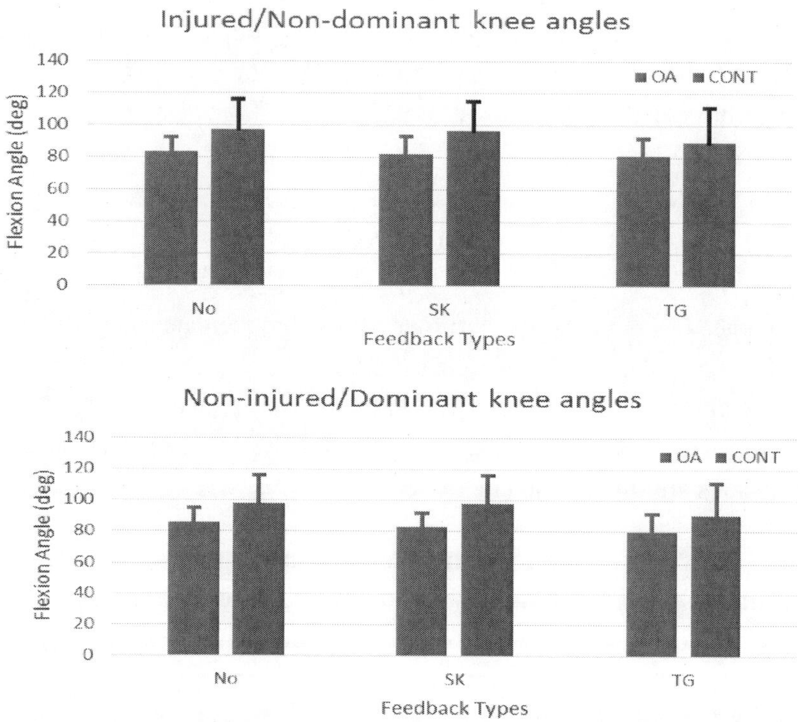

Figure 3. Average peak knee flexion angle. NO, no feedback; SK, kinematic feedback (stick-figure); TG, kinetic feedback (COPnet target).

Knee extension moment

In patients with knee OA, the peak knee extensor moment in the non-injured knee was 0.49 Nm/kg.m with no feedback, 0.47 Nm/kg.m with kinematic feedback and 0.45 Nm/kg.m with kinetic feedback (see Figure 4). In healthy participants, the peak knee extensor moment in the dominant knee was 0.45 Nm/kg.m with no feedback and with kinetic feedback and 0.43 Nm/kg.m with kinematic feedback, and in the non-dominant knee was at least 0.02 Nm/kg.m higher in with kinematic feedback than with no feedback (see Figure 4).

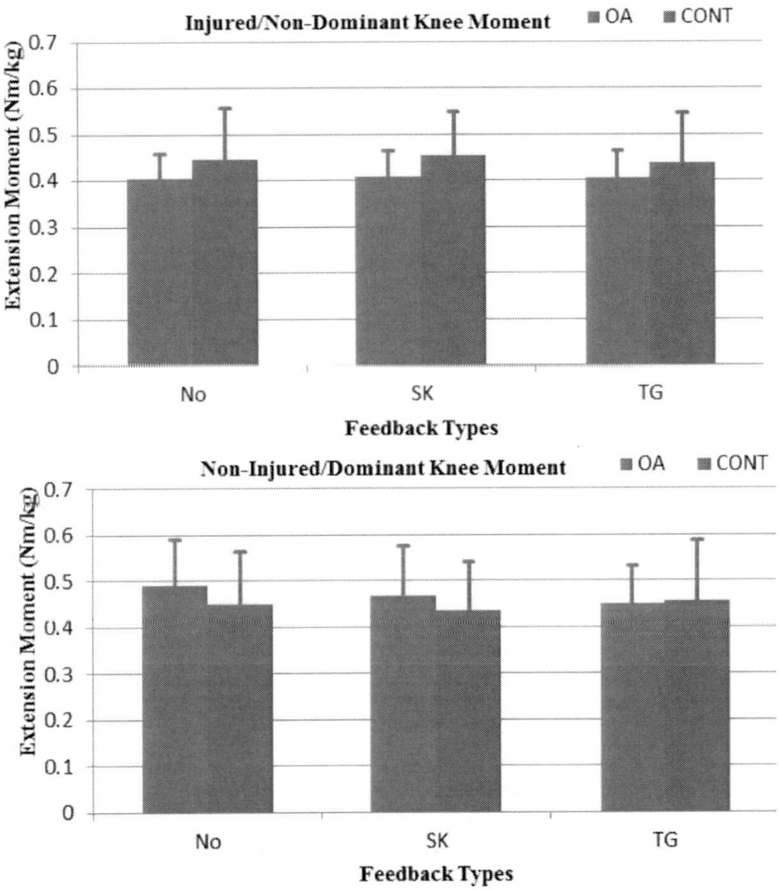

Figure 4. Peakknee extensor moment. Data are the mean of all subjects. Error bars represent standard deviation. NO, no feedback; SK, kinematic feedback (stick-figure); TG, kinetic feedback (COPnet target).

Support moment

In both groups, SYSM was closest to 100% in the kinetic feedback condition. In patients with knee OA, SYSM was higher in the kinematic feedback than in the no feedback condition (93.8%; see Figure 5). This was accompanied by a reduction of at least 1% in the contribution of the injured knee to the total SYSM. However, in healthy participants, SYSM was 104.4% with no feedback and 96.5% with kinematic feedback, which was accompanied by an increase of 4% in the contribution of the dominant knee to the total SYSM (see Figure 5).

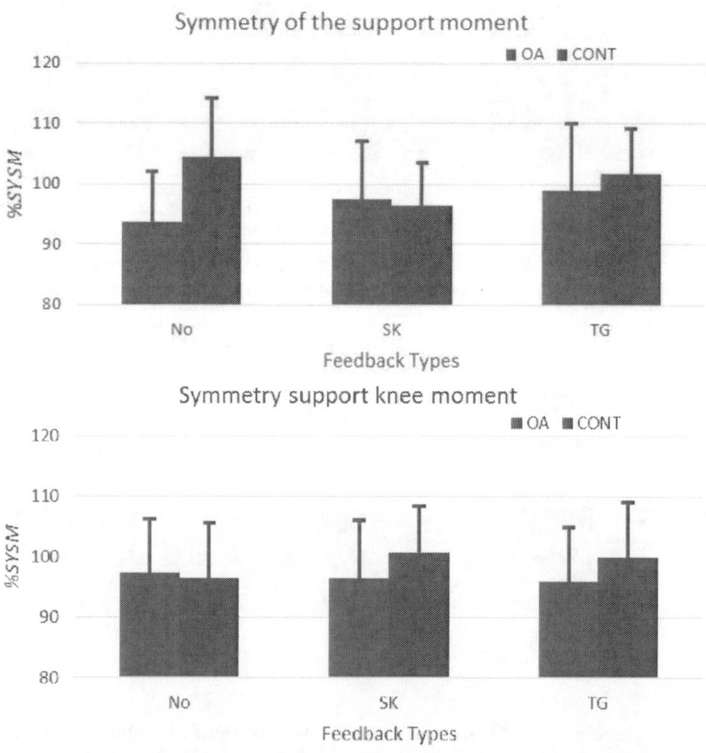

Figure 5. A: The total symmetry of the support moment between injured/dominant and non-injured/non- dominant legs. B: Symmetry support knee moment between injured/dominant and non-injured/non-dominant knees. Error bars represent standard deviation.NO, no feedback; SK, kinematic feedback (stick-figure); TG, kinetic feedback (COPnet target).

Discussion

The overall goal of this study was to explore whether an in-house-developed real-time targeted feedback application influenced healthy and OA individuals' motor control strategies during double-leg squatting. Healthy subjects altered their squatting strategy when provided with kinematic feedback in the form of a stick figure of the lower limbs, as evidenced by a SYSM that was 4% lower than 100% in this condition. This is in line with our previous data (18) that indicated the percentage of total SYSM in healthy subjects changed when they performed a double-leg squat with stick-figure feedback. Patients with knee OA showed a slightly better distribution of the support moment over both legs when provided with kinematic feedback than when provided with no feedback, as evidenced by a SYSM that was 3% less than 100%. To probe this difference between conditions, we investigated extensor knee moments. Healthy subjects reduced the extensor moment in the non-dominant knee and increased the extensor moment in their dominant knee when provided with kinematic feedback, whereas patients with knee OA only altered the extensor moment in their injured knee. This may suggest that healthy subjects focused on the kinematic information presented to alter their body position during the squat as we observed, where patients with knee OA compensated strategies as they might need to improve the presented information of the injured leg.

In both groups of subjects, motor control strategies improved when kinetic feedback was provided. This is evidenced by the comparable distribution over both legs in the two groups. In patients with knee OA, the extensor moment in the injured knee was much smaller in the kinetic feedback condition than in the no feedback and kinematic feedback conditions. This may indicate that the kinetic feedback encouraged them to use their injured knee. In healthy subjects, squat depth (indicated by peak knee flexion angle) was at least 7o lower in the kinetic feedback condition in healthy subjects than in the no feedback and kinematic feedback conditions. By contrast, patients with knee OA maintained a similar squat depth across all three conditions.

Taken together, these preliminary results suggest that both types of feedback may have a greater effect on patients with knee OA than on healthy subjects. The kinetic feedback may be superior to the kinematic feedback for re-educating an individual on how to best perform a double-leg squat. This is not surprising, as the kinematic feedback presented internal information (i.e., the position of body segments or limbs) whereas the kinetic feedback provided an external focus on individuals' movements (25-28). Further data are required to explicate these effects of feedback type on squatting strategy.

The main limitation of this study is the small sample size, and additional data are needed before firm conclusions that be drawn. We did not investigate the percentage of moment support of the hip, knee and ankle in both legs. Although it is believed that these three joints should contribute to the total support moment in similar amounts in both legs as far as it is 100%, but studying all three joints would uncover which joint is the main contributor to the total support moment. Further clinical research is needed to explore if the differences observed are clinically meaningful.

CONCLUSION

In conclusion, the preliminary results of this ongoing research highlight the potential of our real-time targeted feedback to promote subtle alterations in movement strategy during double-leg squatting. If deployed in the clinical setting, the methods outlined herein may improve existing assessment procedures and training techniques for motor control, but further longitudinal research on a larger sample size must be carried out. These preliminary results are very encouraging for our on-going research in which we aim to provide evidence to support this conclusion.

Acknowledgments

The authors would like to thank the volunteers for their time, enthusiasm and feedback.

References

[1] Zhang Y, Jordan JM. Epidemiology of osteoarthritis. Clin Geriatr Med 2010;26(3):355-69.

[2] NICE guidelines. Osteoarthritis: care and management. London: NICE, 2014.

[3] Chacón JG, González NE, Véliz A, Losada BR, Paul H, Santiago LG, et al. Effect of knee osteoarthritis on the perception of quality of life in Venezuelan patients. Arthritis Care Res 2004;51(3):377-82.

[4] Blagojevic M, Jinks C, Jeffery A, Jordan KP. Risk factors for onset of osteoarthritis of the knee in older adults: A systematic review and meta-analysis. Osteoarthritis Cartilage 2010;18(1):24-33.

[5] Page CJ, Hinman RS, Bennell KL. Physiotherapy management of knee osteoarthritis. Int J Rheuma Dis 2011;14(2):145-51.

[6] Bennell KL, Kyriakides M, Metcalf B, Egerton T, Wrigley TV, Hodges PW, et al. Neuromuscular versus quadriceps strengthening exercise in patients with medial knee osteoarthritis and varus malalignment: A randomized controlled trial. Arthritis Rheumatol 2014;66(4):950-9.

[7] Bennell KL, Hall M, Hinman RS. Osteoarthritis year in review 2015: Rehabilitation and outcomes. Osteoarthritis Cartilage. 2016;24(1):58-70.

[8] Tanaka R, Ozawa J, Kito N, Moriyama H. Effects of exercise therapy on walking ability in individuals with knee osteoarthritis: a systematic review and meta-analysis of randomised controlled trials. Clin Rehabil 2016;30(1):36-52.

[9] Lange AK, Vanwanseele B, Fiatarone Singh MA. Strength training for treatment of osteoarthritis of the knee: A systematic review. Arthritis Care Res 2008; 59(10):1488-94.

[10] Shumway-Cook A, Woollacott MH. Motor control: Theory and practical applications. Philadelphia, PA: Lippincott Williams Wilkins, 1995.

[11] Woollacott MH, Shumway-Cook A. Postural dysfunction during standing and walking in children with cerebral palsy: What are the underlying problems and what new therapies might improve balance? Neural Plasticity 2005;12(2-3):211-9.

[12] Bandur A. Self-efficacy: The exercise of control. New York: Worth, 1997.

[13] Vermeire E, Hearnshaw H, Van Royen P, Denekens J. Patient adherence to treatment: three decades of research. A comprehensive review. J Clin Pharm Therapeut 2001;26(5):331-42.

[14] Holden MK. Virtual environments for motor rehabilitation: Review. CyberPsychol Behav 2005;8(3):187-211.

[15] Rizzo A, Kim GJ. A SWOT analysis of the field of virtual reality rehabilitation and therapy. Presence 2005;14(2):119-46.

[16] Gokeler A, Bisschop M, Myer G, Benjaminse A, Dijkstra P, van Keeken H, et al. Immersive virtual reality improves movement patterns in patients after ACL reconstruction: implications for enhanced criteria-based return-to-sport rehabilitation. Knee Surg Sports Traumatol Arthrosc 2014;14:1-7.

[17] Burdea GC, Coiffet P. Virtual reality technology, 2nd ed. New York: Wiley-Blackwell, 2003.

[18] Al-Amri M, Roos PE, Button K, Deursen RV, eds. Virtual reality based double leg squat exercise: Preliminary study. Virtual rehabilitation (ICVR), 2013 International Conference, 2013 Aug 26-29.

[19] Deutsch JE, Brettler A, Smith C, Welsh J, John R, Guarrera-Bowlby P, et al. Nintendo Wii sports and Wii fit game analysis, validation, and application to stroke rehabilitation. Topics Stroke Rehabil 2011;18(6):701-19.

[20] Park D-S, Lee G. Validity and reliability of balance assessment software using the Nintendo Wii balance board: usability and validation. J Neuroeng Rehabil 2014;11:99.

[21] Escamilla RF. Knee biomechanics of the dynamic squat exercise. Med Sci Sports Exercise 2001;33(1):127-41.

[22] Tegner Y, Lysholm J. Rating systems in the evaluation of knee ligament injuries. Clin OrthopaedicsRelat Res 1985;198:43-9.

[23] Winter DA, Patla AE, Prince F, Ishac M, Gielo-Perczak K. Stiffness control of balance in quiet standing. J Neurophysiol 1998;80(3):1211-21.

[24] Winter DA. Biomechanics and motor control of human movement. Hoboken, NJ: John Wiley, 1990.

[25] Wulf G, McConnel N, Gärtner M, Schwarz A. Enhancing the learning of sport skills through external-focus feedback. J Motor Behav 2002;34(2):171-82.

[26] Wulf G, McNevin N. Simply distracting learners is not enough: More evidence for the learning benefits of an external focus of attention. Eur J Sport Sci 2003;3(5):1-13.

[27] Wulf G, Dufek JS, Lozano L, Pettigrew C. Increased jump height and reduced EMG activity with an external focus. Hum Movement Sci 2010;29(3):440-8.

[28] Wulf G. Attentional focus and motor learning: a review of 15 years. Int Rev Sport Exercise Psychol 2013;6(1):77-104.

In: Rehabilitation
Editors: Wendy Powell et al.
ISBN: 978-1-53612-080-6

Chapter 8

COMPARISON OF FUNCTIONAL BENEFITS OF SELF-MANAGEMENT TRAINING FOR AMPUTEES UNDER VIRTUAL WORLD AND E-LEARNING CONDITIONS

Sandra L Winkler*, PhD, OTR/L, John A Kairalla, PhD, Robin Cooper, PhD, Allison Hall, PhD, Michelle Schlesinger, MOT, Alice Krueger and Ann Ludwig
Center of Innovation on Disability and Rehabilitation Research, James A Haley VA Hospital, Tampa, Florida,
College of Public Health and Health Professions and College of Medicine, University of Florida, Gainesville, Florida,
Conflict Resolution Studies Department, Nova Southeastern University, Fort Lauderdale, Florida,

---

* Corresponding author: Sandra L Winkler, PhD, OTR/L, Research Health Science Specialist, Center of Innovation on Disability and Rehabilitation Research, James A Haley VA Hospital, 8900 Grand Oak Circle (151R), Tampa. FL 33637-1022, United States. Email: Sandra.winkler@va.gov.

Occupational Therapy Department, Nova Southeastern University,
Fort Lauderdale, Florida,
Virtual Ability Inc, Aurora, Colorado, US

Amputation is a life-long condition. Throughout their lifespan, amputees will need health, wellness and prosthetic-related information. This project used a randomized design to compare two methods of disseminating an evidence-based self-management intervention: avatar-based virtual world and e-learning environments. Of the 57 subjects randomized, 37 (65%) completed the study. The virtual world group had a significantly higher dropout rate than the e-learning group. Both groups marginally improved on self-efficacy, perceived social support, pain interference, and functional status outcomes with no significant results found between the groups.

INTRODUCTION

Nearly 2 million people live with limb loss in the United States of America (1, 2), with projections to reach 3.6 million persons by 2050 (3). Approximately 185,000 amputations occur in the United States (US) each year (1, 4). However, amputation is not only a US issue, but a global one. For example, in countries such as Angola and Cambodia where land mines are the cause of most traumatic amputations, there are more than 50 amputees per 20,000 people (5). While global amputee prevalence rates are not available, the World Health Organization estimates that more than 30 million people in Africa, Asia, and Latin America combined are in need of prosthetic and other assistive devices (WHO, 2004).

Since amputation is a life-long condition, it is important for those with limb loss to be educated consumers of information about current and evolving medical procedures, prosthetic technologies, rehabilitative interventions, and health and wellness. Prosthetic devices must be provided throughout the lifespan of individuals with amputation. For example, prosthetic devices provided in the United States by the Department of Defence or the Department of Veterans Affairs are typically replaced in less than two years (6). Selecting appropriate prosthetic components can be overwhelming because of emerging technology. In fact, amputees have reported a lack of available information on new prosthetic devices (7). Prevention and treatment of secondary health conditions associated with amputation and prosthetic device use are also needed throughout the lifespan of individuals with amputation, for conditions such as pain (8), skin problems (9-11), heterotopic ossification (7), arthritis (9, 12), cumulative trauma disorders and overuse injuries of the non-involved limb (6), and psychological/mental health issues (13, 14). Individuals with limb loss who feel they are well educated about their amputation care are more likely to adhere to treatment recommendations and have improved health outcomes (7).

Self-management interjects active participation into treatment (15). The effectiveness of self-management programs is attributed not to changes in behaviour, but rather to enhanced self-efficacy or a feeling of control over the illness/disability (16, 17). Programs that teach self-efficacy are more effective in improving clinical outcomes than traditional patient education (18).

The problem that this research addresses is providing access to this self-management education, especially for amputees with mobility and/or geographic barriers. This training was initially designed to assist with community integration for service members with combat-related amputations who had been discharged from specialized rehabilitation and were returning home. The training was extended to non-service member amputees. Guided by Bandura's theoretical model, this project created a virtual world environment in Second Life® (SL; www.secondlife.com), thus expanding interactive dissemination of health and prosthetic-related evidence-based information from face-to-face (clinician to patient) to the Internet (virtual world). A virtual world environment removes travel and accessibility barriers that are particularly challenging for individuals in rural areas and individuals with disabilities (19, 20) and hosts a global audience. The research question asked if being able to observe yourself immersed, as an avatar, in performing balance and conditioning exercises, for example, added value to the training compared to watching video of peers performing the tasks.

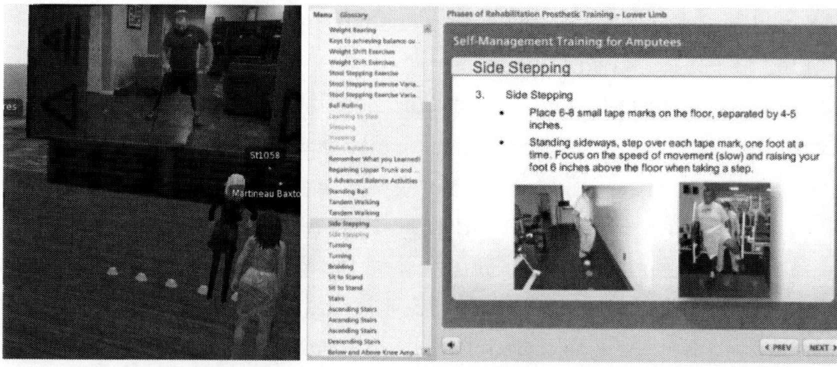

Figure 1. A side-stepping balance exercise in the virtual world condition (left) and the e-learning condition (right).

OUR STUDY

This study had a development and an experimental phase. During the development phase, subject experts created the content of the self-management training based on Alberto Esquenazi's Stages of Rehabilitation for Amputees (21). Using Microsoft PowerPoint as the authoring tool, a visual presentation with accompanying video and still graphics was created and then used by the virtual world and e-learning developers to build the experimental and control conditions, respectively. Content was beta-tested; results have been reported previously (22). The two research environments—virtual world (VW) using SL and e-learning (EL) using Articulate® software (www.articulate.com) - were created based on identical PowerPoint content (see Figure 1).

The experimental phase used a randomized, pre- and post-design to compare the effectiveness of the intervention under two conditions: virtual world and e-learning. The results of the experimental phase are reported in this paper.

Amputee subjects were recruited to participate via IRB-approved flyers with a targeted enrolment of 92. The majority of subjects were recruited from advertisement of the study on the Amputee Coalition website. Inclusion criteria included: major amputation; access to a computer;

functional use of computer (mouse, voice activation software); English-speaking. The only exclusion criterion was finger or toe amputation(s) only. Subjects did not need to be using prostheses to be included in the study. See Table 1 for a comparison of subjects randomized to the experimental and control groups as well as a comparison of those completing the study.

Table 1. Description of sample

		Total Randomized (n = 57)		**Study Completers (n = 37)**	
		VW	**EL**	**VW**	**EL**
		n = 28	**n = 29**	**n = 14**	**n = 23**
Age: mean (sd)		48.7 (14.4)	51.8 (14.9)	50.6 (12.4)	48.4 (13.9)
Race/ethnicity n (%)	White	22 (79)	25 (86)	13 (93)	20 (87)
	Black	4 (14)	1 (3)	1 (7)	1 (4)
	Other	2 (7)	3 (10)	0 (0)	2 (9)
Gender n (%)	Male	18 (64)	18 (62)	11 (79)	15 (65)
	Female	10 (36)	11 (38)	3 (21)	8 (35)
Amputation n (%)	Unilateral UL	2(7)	1 (3)	1 (7)	1 (4)
	Unilateral LL	22 (79)	21(72)	11 (79)	17 (74)
	Bilateral LL	1(4)	5 (17)	1 (7)	3 (13)
	Unilateral UL & Bilateral LL	1(4)	0(0)	1(7)	0(0)
	Unilateral UL & Bilateral LL	0 (0)	1 (3)	0 (0)	1 (4)
	Quad	2 (7)	1 (3)	0 (0)	1 (4)
Years since 1st amputation n (%)	0-5	21 (75)	16 (55)	11 (79)	14 (61)
	6-10	2 (7)	7 (24)	1 (7)	3 (13)
	11-15	1 (4)	4 (14)	1 (7)	4 (17)
	>15	4 (14)	2 (7)	1 (7)	2 (9)
Etiology n (%)	Trauma	9 (32)	12 (41)	5 (36)	11 (48)
	Dysvascular Disease	8 (29)	7 (24)	4 (29)	10 (43)
	Other Medical	11 (39)	10 (34)	5 (36)	2 (9)
Prosthetic use n (%)	Daily	23 (82)	25(86)	10 (71)	19 (83)
	Weekly	0 (0)	2 (7)	0 (0)	2 (9)
	Monthly or less	0 (0)	1 (3)	0 (0)	1 (4)
	Did not use prosthesis	5(18)	1 (3)	4 (29)	1 (4)
On computer	Hours per week	29.6 (15.1)	31.2 (20.2)	28.9 (12.0)	31.8 (20.6)
Mean (sd)					

Theoretical framework

This project was guided by Bandura's self-efficacy theory (23), addressing each of the four sources of self-efficacy: 1) Performance accomplishment/ mastery, 2) Modeling/vicarious experience, 3) Verbal persuasion/ Interpretation of symptoms, and 4) Social persuasion (16, 17). The project was also guided by Kraiger's theory of training evaluation (24) that expands learning outcomes to include cognitive (knowledge, metacognition), skill-based (skill development, ability to apply learned behaviours to new task settings), and affective (self-efficacy) outcomes, all of which are represented in the self-management intervention.

Procedure

After signing the informed consent document, subjects provided baseline demographic information, including protected health information, over the phone. Baseline outcomes data were completed electronically using REDCap, an electronic data capture system hosted at Nova Southeastern University; thus, the investigators were blinded to outcomes data collection. Subjects were then randomized and oriented to either the VW or EL trainings.

Subjects randomized to the EL group received an email with the link to the Articulate® software training. The e-learning presentation content (text and videos) was identical to the virtual world content. The difference was the modality of content delivery. For the EL training, amputees worked alone on their own computer, navigating through the content by menu selections. Only two subjects randomized to the EL training needed assistance, which consisted of instruction to click on the arrow icon to advance the slides.

Subjects randomized to the VW group were oriented by providing them with a manual (by research staff approved by the IRB to have subject contact) that explained how to get a free SL account and avatar, how to log into SL, and the SL location where they would meet a buddy who would train them in SL and how to operate their avatar. Once the subject had an avatar, a the same research staff member met them in SL and introduced them to their "buddy" who provided further training in basic avatar navigation and communication, the subjects were granted access to the research island. This hand off from research staff to "buddy" was important because only the research staff knew the subjects real identity. Once the subject had an avatar, they could be anonymous, as the "buddy" was not authorized by the IRB to have access to protected health information.

The research island had 17 stations with content including the history of prosthetics, the epidemiology of amputation, building prosthetic devices, conditioning and balance exercises, activities of daily living tasks, social emotional adjustment, and community reintegration. The experimental group walked their avatar through the 17 stations, with opportunities to wear virtual prosthetics and participate in virtual simulations, e.g., watching their avatar walk up and down stairs as a bilateral lower limb amputee, and to move through the stations with other amputees (avatars).

Subjects completed the trainings at their own pace. When finished, subjects completed the electronic outcomes assessment, using REDCap, for a second time.

Outcomes

The outcomes were self-efficacy, perceived social support, pain interference, and upper level and lower level limb function.

Self-efficacy was measured using two scales: the General Self-Efficacy Scale (GSE) and the Stanford University School of Medicine Patient Education Chronic Disease Self-Efficacy Scale (25). The 10-item GSE scale assesses a general sense of perceived self-efficacy to predict coping with daily hassles as well as adaptation after experiencing all kinds of stressful life events. The GSE has 10 items with a scale of 1 to 4 each and a possible total mean range from 1-4, with a higher score indicating greater self-efficacy. Six of the 10 Stanford scale items were used. The items each have a scale of 0 to 10 for a possible total mean range from 0-10, with a higher score indicating greater self-efficacy.

Perceived social support was measured using the Multidimensional Scale of Perceived Social Support (MSPSS) (26). The MSPSS measures the perceived availability of support. The MSPSS has 12 items each with a Likert-type scale of 1 to 7 for a possible total mean range from 1-7; a higher score indicates greater perceived social support.

Pain Interference was measured using the "Pain Interference" component of the West Haven-Yale Multidimensional Pain Inventory (WHYMPI) (27) . The WHYMPI is a 52-item, 12-scale inventory that is divided into three parts. Part I includes five scales designed to measure important dimensions of the chronic pain experience including; 1) perceived interference of pain in vocational, social/recreational, and family/marital functioning, 2) support or concern from spouse or significant other, 3) pain severity, 4) perceived life control, and 5) affective distress. Part II assesses patients' perceptions of the degree to which spouses or significant others display Solicitous, Distracting or Negative responses to their pain behaviours and complaints. Part III assesses patients' report of the frequency with which they engage in four categories of common everyday activities; Household Chores, Outdoor Work, Activities Away from Home, and Social Activities. Only the nine items assessing the interference pain has on subjects' lives and their levels of affective distress were used in this study. The nine WHYMPI items each have a Likert-type scale of 0 to 6 for a possible total mean range from 0-6; a higher score indicates greater pain interference.

Functional Status was measured using the Orthotics Prosthetics User's Survey (OPUS) (28-30). The Orthotics and Prosthetics Users' Survey (OPUS) is a patient-reported outcome measure consisting of five modules assessing Lower Extremity Functional Status (LEFS), Upper Extremity Functional Status (UEFS), Client Satisfaction with Device, Client Satisfaction with Services, and, Health-Related Quality of Life. Only the LEFS and/or UEFS modules (whichever were appropriate for the subject) were used in this study. The LEFS has 20 items each with a Likert-type scale of 1 to 5 for a possible mean range from 1-5; a higher score indicates better function. The UEFS has 28 items each with a Likert-type scale of 1 to 5 for a possible mean range from 1-5; a higher score indicates better function.

Data analysis

Descriptive statistics of the sample for both randomized subjects and study completers by group include race, gender, amputation type, time since amputation, etiology, prosthetic use frequency, and computer usage. Frequencies for categorical variables and means (standard deviation) for continuous variables are presented. For outcome measures, baseline outcomes were subtracted from post-treatment scores in order to create change scores. Change scores for the two groups were tested using two-sided Wilcoxon rank sum tests. A significance level of 0.05 was used for all tests.

FINDINGS

Of the 59 subjects enrolled, 57 were randomized: 28 to the VW experimental group and 29 to the EL control group. Of the 57 subjects randomized, 37 (65%) completed the study. The VW group had a significantly higher drop-out rate; 14/28 (50%) of the VW group dropped out while 6/29 (21%) of the EL group dropped out ($p = 0.02$).

Table 1 compares characteristics of the VW (experimental) and EL (control) groups. While the dropout rate was high for the study (35% overall), measurable demographic differences were not found between study completers and dropouts, with only a trend towards newer amputees being more likely to complete the study. Randomization groups were comparable both overall and when comparing only completers.

Table 2. Comparison of pre and post change in outcomes scores for the virtual world (VW) and e-learning (EL) groups

Outcomes	n	VW (n=14)			ES+	n	EL (n=23)			ES	P value
		Pre	Post	Change			Pre	Post	Change		
Self-efficacy (GSE)	14	3.54	3.56	0.03	0.11	23	3.48	3.49	0.01	0.05	0.97
Self-efficacy (SSE)	14	8.68	8.85	0.17	0.15	23	8.04	7.97	-0.07	-0.06	0.80
Social support	14	5.38	5.62	0.24	0.30	23	5.91	6.00	0.09	0.11	0.56
Pain interference#	9	2.05	1.85	-0.20	-0.21	19	3.28	3.10	-0.17	-0.18	0.75
Lower limb function^	11	3.34	3.44	0.10	0.37	20	3.23	3.33	0.10	0.37	0.87
Upper limb function*	2	3.13	3.00	-0.13	-0.37	3	2.75	2.86	0.11	0.31	---

+ Effect Size, mean change divided by the pooled standard deviation of change scores

Pain Interference: Lower scores indicate less interference

^ Lower Limb Function: 4 subjects excluded due to data entry errors

* Upper Limb function was not tested due to small sample size (n = 5)

Table 2 displays the change in self-efficacy, perceived social support, pain interference, and upper and lower limb functioning for the control and experimental groups. Both groups descriptively benefited from the self-management training, with small increases observed in self-efficacy, increases in social support, decreases in pain interference, and increases in lower limb function. While the VW group showed slightly better improvements, when using two-sided Wilcoxon rank sum tests to compare the groups on change scores, no statistically significant differences were observed.

DISCUSSION

This project compared the dissemination of a self-management training for amputees under two conditions: virtual world and e-learning. The difference between the two conditions was that the subjects in the avatar-based VW group were immersed in the training, engaging in simulations of desired health activities, e.g., performing activities of daily living transfers, conditioning and balance exercises, going up and down stairs, etc. Small benefits from the self-management training were observed for both groups across the outcomes considered. However, no statistically significant differences were observed between the groups.

The original study plan called for a total enrolment of n = 100 in order to achieve 92 evaluable subjects, and was powered to detect moderate effect sizes of 0.6. Unfortunately, the enrolment rate was less than expected and dropout rates were higher than expected. Additionally, the dropout rate for the VW group was significantly larger than for the EL group. Because of the lower than expected enrolment and high dropout rate (50% in the VW group and 21% in the EL group), the study was underpowered to detect a significant difference unless large effect sizes were observed. The reasons for subjects dropping out of the SL group varied. One subject believed that the SL software was a virus and took his computer to a repair shop to have it removed. Two to three two subjects (out of the 57 randomized) did not have an adequate graphic card to run SL. A couple of older subjects (aged over 80) were frustrated with the technology. Two of the three amputees with loss of all four limbs had difficulty with navigation; the third completed the study using voice recognition software. Several amputees were just too busy to complete 17 stations: these amputees were working, raising children, engaged in sports, etc. In reflection, the training was comprehensive but probably too long. Most drops outs went into the virtual world once or twice, but not the multiple times needed to complete the study. That being said, one or two subjects completed the 17 virtual world stations in one or two sessions. Only one amputee reported not feeling safe in a virtual world. Recruitment was also affected by the nature of the intervention; many amputees who inquired about the study did not enrol. Subjects reported wanting to participate in studies if it helped other amputees, but were perhaps negatively influenced about having to participate in the study as an avatar. Younger subjects who were familiar with avatars seemed to complete the intervention more easily and quickly.

There were limitations with the way that two of the outcomes measures, pain interference and function, were used in this study. Pain interference data was excluded for nine subjects because seven subjects put not applicable for all items pre/post, one put not applicable for all items post, and one had pre, but rated seven out of nine items not applicable on the post test. Future studies will include a clarifying item: I have pain, yes or no, and then ask subjects who have pain to complete the pain interference questions.

Additionally, there was confusion for the upper and lower limb functioning questionnaire that led to further data loss. Each participant has access to complete both measures, regardless of amputation type. While not applicable was a choice that many correctly used, others inadvertently filled out incorrect portions. Specifically, two participants did not complete the pre-test, one did not complete the post-test, and two other completed the pre-test for upper limb function, but not for lower limb function. Contributing to this confusion was the investigators' use of electronic data collection for the first time. Although the electronic forms were piloted before use, future studies will include more extensive pilot testing prior to implementation.

In general, the amputees most likely to complete the virtual world training were new amputees; in fact, several subjects' avatars were wearing virtual prostheses before they received their real life or non-virtual prostheses. Notably, dropouts had lower baseline pain interference (less pain interference) on average than completers (Wilcoxon two-sided $p = 0.024$), suggesting that dropout could be related to less need for therapy. The study results suggest that the virtual world training may be most appropriate for amputees who are receiving inpatient and outpatient rehabilitation, do not have access to rehabilitation, want to connect with other amputees, and want to experience activities that they can no longer do post-amputation. In a current project, this research team is adding a self-management training for diabetics at risk for foot ulcers; participants will have an opportunity to interact with amputees who have experienced diabetes-related amputations.

Conclusion

Amputees in the e-learning and virtual world groups benefited somewhat from the self-management training. The results suggest that the virtual world training may be most appropriate for amputees who do not have access to rehabilitation and as an adjunct to inpatient and outpatient rehabilitation, especially for amputees who want to connect with other amputees or experience activities that they can no longer do post-amputation(s).

Acknowledgments

We would like to thank all the individuals with limb differences who participated in this project. This project is supported by the Agency for Healthcare Research and Quality Award # R24HS022021, PI Sandra Winkler, 2013-2017.

REFERENCES

[1] ACA. Limb Loss Statistics [web page]. Amputee Coalition of America, 2012. URL http:// www.amputee-coalition.org/ limb-loss-information/ limb-loss-statistics/index.html.

[2] Ziegler-Graham K, MacKenzie EJ, Ephraim PL, Travison TG, Brookmeyer R. Estimating the prevalence of limb loss in the United States: 2005 to 2050. Arch Phys Med Rehabil 2008; 89(3): 422-9.

[3] Ziegler-Graham K, Mackenzie EJ, Ephraim PL, Travison TG, Brookmeyer R. Estimating the prevalence of limb loss in the United States: 2005-2050. Arch Phys Med Rehabil 2008; 89(3): 422-9.

[4] CDC. Ambulatory and inpatient procedures in the United States, 1996. Washington DC: US Department of Health and Human Services, 1998.

[5] Landmines: The facts. New Internationalist 1997 Sept 05.

[6] McFarland LV, Hubbard Winkler SL, Jones MW, Heinemann AW, Esquenazi A, et al. Unilateral upper limb prosthetic use, satisfaction and abandonment in service members from Vietnam and OIF/OEF conflicts with major traumatic limb loss. J Rehabil Res Dev 2010; 47(4): 299-316.

[7] Berke GM, Fergason J, Milani JR, Hattingh J, McDowell M, Nguyen V, et al. Comparison of satisfaction with current prosthetic care in veterans and servicemembers from Vietnam and OIF/OEF conflicts with major traumatic limb loss. J Rehabil Res Dev 2010; 47(4): 361-71.

[8] Ehde DM, Czerniecki JM, Smith DG, Campbell KM, Edwards WT, Jensen MP, et al. Chronic phantom sensations, phantom pain, residual limb pain, and other regional pain after lower limb amputation. Arch Phys Med Rehabil 2000; 81(8): 1039-44.

[9] Reiber GE, McFarland LV, Hubbard S, Maynard C, Blough DK, Gambel JM, et al. Servicemembers and veterans with major traumatic limb loss from Vietnam war and OIF/OEF conflicts: survey methods, participants, and summary findings. J Rehabil Res Dev 2010; 47(4): 275-97.

[10] Bui KM, Raugi GJ, Nguyen VQ, Reiber GE. Skin problems in individuals with lower-limb loss: literature review and proposed classification system. J Rehabil Res Dev 2009; 46(9): 1085-90.

[11] Meulenbelt HE, Geertzen JH, Dijkstra PU, Jonkman MF. Skin problems in lower limb amputees: an overview by case reports. J Eur Acad Dermatol Venereol 2007; 21(2): 147-55.

[12] Norvell DC, Czerniecki JM, Reiber GE, Maynard C, Pecoraro JA, Weiss NS. The prevalence of knee pain and symptomatic knee osteoarthritis among veteran traumatic amputees and nonamputees. Arch Phys Med Rehabil 2005; 86(3): 487-93.

[13] Ostlie K, Magnus P, Skjeldal OH, Garfelt B, Tambs K. Mental health and satisfaction with life among upper limb amputees: a Norwegian population-based survey comparing adult acquired major upper limb amputees with a control group. Disabil Rehabil 2011; 33(17-18): 1594-607.

[14] Horgan O, MacLachlan M. Psychosocial adjustment to lower-limb amputation: a review. Disabil Rehabil 2004; 26(14-15): 837-50.

[15] Creer T, Renne C, Christian W. Behaviorial contributions to rehabilitation and childhood asthma. Rehabil Literature 1976; 37: 226-32.

[16] Lorig K, Holman HR. Self-management education: history, definition, outcomes, mechanisms. Ann Behav Med 2003; 26(1): 1-7.

[17] Bandura A. Self-efficacy: The exercise of control. New York: WHFreeman, 1977.

[18] Bodenheimer T, Lorig K, Holman HR, Grumbach K. Patient self-management of chronic disease in primary care. JAMA 2002; 288: 2469-75.

[19] Chan L, Hart LG, Goodman DC. Geographic access to health care for rural Medicare beneficiaries. J Rural Health 2006; 22(2): 140-6.

[20] Guagliardo MF. Spatial accessibility of primary care: concepts, methods and challenges. Int J Health Geographics 2004; 3(1): 3.

[21] Esquenazi A. Amputation rehabilitation and prosthetic restoration. From surgery to community reintegration. Disabil Rehabil 2004; 26(14): 831-6.

[22] Winkler SL, Cooper R, Kraiger K, Gaunaurd I, Fisher A, Kairalla J, et al. Self-management intervention for amputees in a virtual world environment. In: Sharkey P, Merrick J, eds. Recent advances on using virtual reality technology for rehabilitation. New York: Nova Science, 2016: 25-32.

[23] Bandura A. Self-efficacy: Toward a unifying theory of behavioral change. Psychol Rev 1977; 84: 191-215.

[24] Kraiger K, Ford JK, Salas E. Application of cognitive, skill-based, and affective theories of learning outcomes to new methods of training evaluation. J Appl Psychol 1993; 78(2): 311-28.

[25] Lorig K, Stewart A, Ritter PL, Gonzalez V, Laurent D, Lynch J. Outcome measures for health education and other health care interventions. Thousand Oaks, CA: Sage, 1996.

[26] Zimet GD, Powell SS, Farley GK, Werkman S, Berkoff KA. Psychometric characteristics of the Multidimensional Scale of Perceived Social Support. J Pers Assess 1990; 55(3-4): 610-7.

[27] Kerns RD, Turk DC, Rudy TE. The West Haven-Yale Multidimensional Pain Inventory (WHYMPI). Pain 1985; 23(4): 345-56.

[28] Burger H, Franchignoni F, Heinemann AW, Kotnik S, Giordano A. Validation of the orthotics and prosthetics user survey upper extremity functional status module in people with unilateral upper limb amputation. J Rehabil Med 2008; 40(5): 393-9.

[29] Jarl GM, Heinemann AW, Norling Hermansson LM. Validity evidence for a modified version of the Orthotics and Prosthetics Users' Survey. Disabil Rehabil Assist Technol 2012; 7(6): 469-78.

[30] Heinemann AW, Bode RK, O'Reilly C. Development and measurement properties of the Orthotics and Prosthetics Users' Survey (OPUS): A comprehensive set of clinical outcome instruments. Prosther Orthot Int 2003; 27: 191-206.

In: Rehabilitation
Editors: Wendy Powell et al.
ISBN: 978-1-53612-080-6

Chapter 9

EXPANDED SENSE OF POSSIBILITIES: QUALITATIVE FINDINGS FROM A VIRTUAL SELF-MANAGEMENT TRAINING FOR AMPUTEES

Robin Cooper, PhD, Sandra L Winkler**, PhD, OTR/L,
John Kairalla, PhD, Allison Hall, PhD,
Michelle Schlesinger, MOT,
Alice Krueger and Ann Ludwig
Conflict Resolution Studies Department,
Nova Southeastern University, Fort Lauderdale, Florida
Center of Innovation on Disability and Rehabilitation Research,
James A Haley VA Hospital, Tampa, Florida
Department of Biostatistics, University of Florida, Gainesville, Florida,
Occupational Therapy Department,
Nova Southeastern University, Fort Lauderdale, Florida
Virtual Ability Inc, Aurora, Colorado, US

* Corresponding author: Sandra L Winkler, PhD, OTR/L, Research Health Science Specialist, Center of Innovation on Disability and Rehabilitation Research, James A Haley VA Hospital, 8900 Grand Oak Circle (151R), Tampa. FL 33637-1022, United States. Email: Sandra.winkler@va.gov.

This chapter presents the procedures and results of a qualitative study that was part of a larger study comparing two methods of accessing a self-management training for amputees: e-learning and a virtual world. Interviews were conducted in Second Life (SL) with fourteen subjects who completed the training in the virtual world and six subjects who completed e-learning training. Interpretative Phenomenological Analysis (IPA) was used for qualitative data analysis, leading to the identification of 14 themes within five major categories. An overarching theme of the SL experience resulting from analysis was that of an expanded sense of possibilities.

INTRODUCTION

In 2004, the Department of Veterans Affairs (VA) convened a traumatic amputation QUERI (Quality Enhancement Research Initiative) workshop to develop best practices for the new generation of war-wounded service members arriving with major limb amputations from the wars in Iraq and Afghanistan. The problem was community reintegration: when the service members returned to their hometowns and local VA medical centers, they did not fit the treatment profile of the typical amputees with amputation(s) resulting from deconditioning diseases. An additional challenge was there were few Iraq and Afghanistan amputees, which meant geographically they were far apart. The distance limited peer interactions and clinician specialty skills. It became apparent at the amputation QUERI workshop that peer support for this cohort of amputees was going to have to be conducted over the Internet. Tele-rehabilitation was an option for specialized regional amputee rehabilitation centers to provide training for more rural clinicians. The virtual world was an option for peer-to-peer interaction and self-management training. The US Department of Defense had built two virtual worlds: one for post-traumatic stress disorder (PTSD) (T2 Virtual PTSD Experience) and the Amputee Virtual Environment Support Space (AVESS). As of 2016, the T2 Virtual PTSD Experience remains active. When the AVESS project lost funding, Dr. Winkler's research team, which included some of the original AVESS team members, built "Virtual Health Adventures" with virtual meeting spaces and self-management education for amputees. It is intended that "Virtual Health Adventures" would be expanded to provide similar experiences for individuals with other disabilities and their families, for example, with diabetic foot ulcers and caregivers of individuals with traumatic brain injury.

A virtual world is a synchronous, computer-based simulated environment, populated by a persistent network of people represented by personalized avatars that simultaneously and independently explore the virtual world, participate in its activities and communicate with others (1-3). Users, through their avatars, are able to socialize, communicate, collaborate and learn with other avatar participants in a three-dimensional environment (4). Second Life® (SL) is the largest of many virtual worlds. Conceptualized by Philip Rosedale who founded Linden Lab, SL offers a persistent, open, unlimited, highly customizable space. The content of SL is created by its users who rent virtual land ("islands"). The result is a shared space that provides a sense of "being with others," seeing physical representations of each other, and communicating and acting in that shared space (5).

Amputation is a permanent condition. Increased prosthetic use is significantly associated with better psychological ($P < .05$) and social health ($P < .001$) (6), but prostheses and prosthetic needs change over time so that acquiring current and evolving prosthetic and health-related information is an ongoing educational process. In addition, social and physical function, and support from others have been identified as important factors in the amputation adjustment process (7). To address these issues, a self-management program was developed. Self-management programs provide patients with the knowledge, skills, and confidence to deal with disease-related problems, e.g., to help patients with managing life roles, negative emotions, comorbidity and secondary conditions (8). The question for this project was: How do amputees view engaging in a self-management training program as an avatar? For example, how do amputees view themselves as an avatar performing conditioning and balance activities? The research presented here was part of a larger study that compared two methods of accessing a self-management training for amputees: e-learning using

Articulate® software (www.articulate.com) and the SL virtual world. We hypothesized that the virtual world cohort would have better health-related outcomes than the less-immersed e-learning group. The purpose of this paper is to present the findings of the qualitative arm of the study aimed at understanding how amputee subjects experienced SL. The research question asked, "How do participants experience the SL virtual world?"

Table 1. Description of sample

		SL n = 14	**e-learning n = 6**
Age	Years (sd)	51.2 (12.5)	57.3 (18.1)
Race/ethnicity	White	14	5
	Black	0	1
Gender	Male	11	3
	Female	3	3
Amputation	Unilateral UL	2	0
	Unilateral LL	11	4
	Bilateral LL	1	1
	Unilateral UL & Bilateral LL	0	1
Years since first amputation	0-5	10	4
	6-10	1	1
	11-15	1	1
	16-20	1	0
	>20	1	0
Etiology	Trauma	5	1
	Dysvascular	3	0
	Disease	6	5
Prosthetic use	Daily	10	5
	Weekly	0	1
	Did not use prosthesis	4	0
On computer	Hours/Week (sd)	28.0 (12.6)	26.2 (16.9)
Prior experience with VW	Count (%)	1 (7%)	0 (0%)

OUR STUDY

Following Institutional Review Board approval at Nova Southeastern University, two islands in SL were rented from Linden Lab on which a self-management training sequence, based on Alberto Esquenazi's Stages of Rehabilitation for Amputees (9), was created. Development of the 17-station self-management training area and virtual world community management were performed by Virtual Ability, Inc.

Participation in a semi-structured interview was included in the informed consent document for the larger study. Because the interviews were held in SL for the purpose of anonymity and confidentiality, all amputee subjects randomized to the virtual world group who completed the study training were invited to participate in the interviews. Amputee subjects completing the study randomized to the control e-learning group were invited to experience the virtual world intervention as an avatar after completing their e-learning training. This group of six amputee subjects were invited to participate in the interview, giving a total of 20 interviews included for analysis in this paper. No subjects declined the interview. See Table 1 for a description of subjects who participated in the semi-structured interviews.

Theoretical approach

The methodology employed for the qualitative component of this study was that of Interpretative Phenomenological Analysis (IPA) (Smith, 2009). With its focus on lived experience and interpretation of meaning, IPA has broad applicability across the social, health and human sciences. In particular, phenomenology is increasingly being used by occupational therapists and occupational scientists as an approach to understand the individual's unique experience within the context of his or her environment (Clarke, 2008). With its focus on understanding experience and meaning, this approach is well suited to evaluating participants' experiences with the virtual environment space. The IPA approach is inductive and iterative in nature, allowing ideas and themes to emerge from the participants' personal accounts rather than imposing a predetermined theory. However, the theoretical framework for the methodology itself is one that draws upon and links phenomenology, hermeneutics, and idiography, as the approach focuses on lived experience, emphasizes the role of interpretation, and acknowledges the significance of individual experience (Cooper, 2014).

Procedure

Subjects were invited to participate in the semi-structured interviews by PI Winkler upon completion of post-training data collection. Interviews were performed in SL by Al Hall, as part of his doctoral research, or by R. Cooper. PI Winkler met subjects in SL then invited them to the virtual conference room where they were introduced to Hall and/or Cooper, through their avatars. Interviews were performed using the text chat feature. The text served as the interview transcript.

Analysis

Co-I Cooper conducted the qualitative data analysis. Data analysis in IPA includes the following steps: a) reading and re-reading of the transcript; b) initial noting and coding of the data; c) developing emergent themes; d) searching for connections across emergent themes; e) moving to the next case; f) looking for patterns across cases; g) developing a theoretical structural description of the experience (Smith, 2009). Initial noting includes three stages of coding in which the researcher notes descriptive, linguistic, and conceptual comments throughout the transcript. Each stage of noting has its own purpose and focus: descriptive comments capture what the participant has experienced; linguistic comments convey the participant's meaning-making process through linguistic indicators such as metaphors, repetition, or capitalization for emphasis; and conceptual comments identify initial possible themes and patterns in a tentative manner, subject to further analysis and interpretation. The themes developed through IPA analysis reflect the focus on experience and meaning, as illustrated below in the results section.

FINDINGS

Analysis of the qualitative data collected through interviews in SL resulted in the development of 14 themes within 5 major categories. The 5 major categories were: 1) General Experience of Second Life; 2) Experience of Using Avatar; 3) Experience of Training Format; 4) Perceptions of Training Content; and 5) Perceptions of Training Needs of Friends and Family. Between 2 and 4 themes were grouped under each of these categories. In presenting these themes below, words in quotation marks are taken directly from participants in order to retain their voice, in keeping with standards of qualitative reporting.

General experience of second life

Theme 1. "Learning curve"

Participants found that it took some practice to become comfortable navigating within Second Life. For almost all participants, this was their first experience in a virtual world. Several noted that they found the Second Life technology somewhat difficult, whether logging in or finding locations. Participants noted that it became easier to maneuver within Second Life with practice.

Theme 2. "An amazing experience"

Participants expressed overwhelmingly positive emotions about their experiences in Second Life. In spite of the learning curve and technical difficulties referred to above, participants used very positive language to express their feelings about their experience in Second Life, including "fun," "thrilling," "intriguing," "amazing," "incredible," and "novel."

Theme 3. Second life a freeing environment

In addition to finding Second Life fun and intriguing, participants spoke of it as an environment that provided a "release" from life in the real world. Several participants noted that spending time in Second Life was an "escape," and referred to wanting to visit more often. Participants noted that one can get "lost" in Second Life, both in terms of not being familiar with the sites they visited, and also in terms of becoming so absorbed in the virtual world that they lost track of how much time was passing. Several participants spoke about the ability to do things in Second Life that they could not do in real life, and the "freedom" they felt.

Experience of using avatar

Theme 4. An enjoyable challenge

Although some participants spoke of having difficulty maneuvering the avatar, they enjoyed using one. The challenges most frequently referred to were dressing the avatar and sitting down. Several participants spoke of enjoying doing things through the avatar that they could not do in real life, such as flying. Several participants noted that they liked the experience of going through the training as an avatar.

Theme 5. Identification with the avatar

Participants found great significance in using an avatar. Several noted that they like the "idea of having an avatar." Participants expressed strong identification with their avatars. One stated, "I felt like the avatar was me." Several stated that seeing their avatar with all four limbs made them feel "normal" or "like a whole person." One participant referred to liking "seeing legs again."

Theme 6. Expanded sense of possibilities

In addition to identifying with the avatar, participants seemed to find inspiration from the avatar's actions. Participants felt less limited as a result of using the avatar. One noted that seeing the avatar "reinforced that I don't have limits." Another commented that he could be fearless as an avatar. Several participants observed that they wished they could do in real life what they could do as an avatar in Second Life. As one participant commented, "I liked being able to do things that I can't do in the real world." One participant perceived the avatar's mobility as transferable to real life, noting "The mobility of the avatar actually transfers to you if you allow it to."

Experience of training format

Theme 7. An interactive training experience

Participants spoke repeatedly of how they appreciated the interactive format of the training in Second Life. Particular interactive aspects of the training that stood out to participants included teleporting to the stations and following the arrows to move through the training. Participants really enjoyed the activities included in the training; some of those mentioned included the car, the cane and the zip line. One participant commented that due to the interactive nature of the training, he felt as though he were really there, going through the course.

Theme 8. Mixed experience with training videos

Participants had both positive and negative experiences related to the videos included in the training. While participants indicated they were glad there were videos in the training, several noted that the videos didn't load or were blurry. Several participants commented that they enjoyed listening to the amputees on the videos. One participant shared that he liked "sitting" as an avatar watching the videos on the big screen.

Perceptions of training content

Theme 9. Complete and educational

Participants found the information in the training to be comprehensive. Participants noted that they found the training interesting, and were able to refer to specific examples of information they recalled that they had found useful or interesting. A majority of participants volunteered that they most enjoyed the information about the history of prosthetics.

Theme 10. Best for new amputees

Participants indicated that they felt the training content was best suited for new amputees. Those who were new amputees expressed appreciated for gaining a better understanding of what to expect. Those who have been amputees for some years spoke of knowing much of the information but finding "reinforcement" in that information.

Theme 11. Positive outcomes

Participants felt they benefited from the training content. Many noted that they had learned a lot; examples cited included ways to put on a prosthesis, ways to do leg exercises, and how to button a shirt with one hand. A few indicated that the training gave them "a good outlook." Several participants shared that the training gave them an expanded sense of options and possibilities.

Theme 12. A transformational experience

Within the category that summarized results pertaining to Perceptions of Training Content, a significant result was that several participants indicated that they found the training in Second Life to be a transformational experience. In referring to the sequence of training stations in SL, one participant commented, "It felt as though I left home and actually took on the course." Many noted that they had applied what they learned in real life. Examples cited included stump care and walking on an uneven surface. A participant noted that following this experience, "I see myself just meeting the challenge without hesitation and resolving any issues by breaking them down. It is easy to be aggressive and without fear in SL." Several noted that participating in the training gave them a sense of connection with other amputees. One participant stated that the training gave him the strength to look at his amputation incision for the first time.

Perceptions of training needs of friends and family

Theme 13. Understanding the challenges of the amputee

Participants indicated that friends and family need training that would provide a better understanding of the challenges amputees face, including how difficult it can be to function with a prosthetic device and issues of daily life. Friends and families need to understand all the stages a person with limb loss goes through. Participants noted that friends and family need training not only on the content in this training but also on the emotional needs of the amputee. One participant suggested it would be beneficial to have a site on Second Life where friends and family could learn together.

Theme 14. Knowing when and how to help

A repeated observation of participants was that friends and family need to learn when and how to help the amputee. Participants indicated friends and family need to learn how to be more patient, and how to talk to the amputee. Participants also suggested practical training such as how to help an amputee who falls, or how to help an amputee up the stairs.

Discussion

In this chapter, we have presented the results of the qualitative portion of a larger study that compared two methods of accessing a self-management training for amputees: e-learning using Articulate® software and the SL virtual world. The qualitative study consisted of 20 individual interviews in which participants responded to open-ended questions related to their experience of completing the training and the meaning they found in engaging in SL. Interpretative Phenomenological Analysis was selected as the appropriate methodology in order to focus on lived experience from an interpretive and idiographic perspective. Data analysis led to the identification of 14 themes, grouped within 5 major categories. In this paper, we presented five categories of themes which together shared the common superordinate category: Expanded Sense of Possibilities. These possibilities were not limited to the amputees themselves, but included family and friends as well.

Through the vivid words of participants as they described their experiences and shared their perceptions of completing the self-management training, it could be seen that they found SL to be a freeing environment, that they identified with their avatars and found that using the avatar gave them a sense of new possibilities, which led to the training being a transformational experience that impacted them in real life. We close with the following quote of one participant, which captures the spirit of the participants collectively in terms of the broader impacts of their experience of training in SL:

> *I looked at myself and realized I need to get active. That I need to acknowledge that this is not a novelty. It is very real and how am I going to make my life better. What am I going to implement to make my life work. For example, I have my old leg and liners, etc. just sitting around my room. That's not what I do with my other stuff. I need to get it organized. Also on a daily basis I need to not be afraid to walk without thinking that every step might mean I'm going to fall. I look at young people and they can do it. It's a mindset that I am working on adopting for myself as I move forward.*

ACKNOWLEDGMENTS

We would like to thank all the participants in this study. This project is supported by the Agency for Healthcare Research and Quality Award # R24HS022021, PI Sandra Winkler, 2013-2017. We dedicate this paper to Al Hall, the PhD student who conducted the majority of the interviews as part of his doctoral research. Sadly, Al is no longer with us to witness the results of his work, but we are indebted to him for his contribution.

REFERENCES

[1] Bartle R. Designing virtual worlds. San Francisco, CA: New Riders, 2003.

[2] Aichner T, Jacob F. Measuring the degree of corporate social media use. Int J Market Res 2015; 57(2): 257-75.

[3] Bell M. Toward a definition of virtual worlds. J Virtual Worlds Res 2008; 1(1).

[4] Ducheneaut N, Wen MH, Yee N, Wadley G, eds. Body and mind: A study of avatar personalization in three virtual worlds. 27th International Conference on Human Factors in Computing Systems, Boston, MA, 2009.

[5] Thomas D, Brown JS. Why virtual worlds can matter. Int J Learn Media 2009; 1(1): 37-49.

[6] Gallagher P, Maclachlan M. The trinity amputation and prosthesis experience scales and quality of life in people with lower-limb amputation. Arch Phys Med Rehabil 2004; 85(5): 730-6.

[7] Gallagher P, Maclachlan M. Adjustment to an artificial limb: a qualitative perspective. J Health Psychol 2001; 6(1): 85-100.

[8] Lorig KR, Sobel DS, Ritter PL, Laurent D, Hobbs M. Effect of a self-management program on patients with chronic disease. Eff Clin Pract 2001; 4: 56-62.

[9] Esquenazi A. Amputation rehabilitation and prosthetic restoration. From surgery to community reintegration. Disabil Rehabil 2004; 26(14): 831-6.

In: Rehabilitation
Editors: Wendy Powell et al.
ISBN: 978-1-53612-080-6

Chapter 10

DESIGN OF A LOCATION-AWARE AUGMENTED AND ALTERNATIVE COMMUNICATION SYSTEM TO SUPPORT PEOPLE WITH LANGUAGE AND SPEECH DISORDERS

M Sazzad Hossain*[*], *BSc*, *Masato Takanokura*, *PhD* and *Kenichi Nakashima*, *PhD
Graduate School of Engineering, Course of Industrial Engineering and Management, Kanagawa University, Kanagawa-Ku, Yokohama, Japan

Working with people who have speech and language disorders can be a great challenge for researchers. Language difficulties can significantly affect a user's ability to communicate with others. If we can develop a system with advantages like location-awareness, messaging, and localization, then it will become more attractive for users. Therefore, it is necessary to develop such a system. Our aim is to design an Augmentative and Alternative Communication (AAC) system based on current location for people with language disorders in order to support communication in

[*] Correspondence: M Sazzad Hossain, Graduate School of Engineering, Course of Industrial Engineering & Management, Kanagawa University, 3-27-1, Rokkakubashi, Kanagawa-ku, Yokohama, 221-8686, Japan. Email: sazzadjoy@gmail.com.

their everyday life. In this chapter, we design and develop a location based AAC system that provides a list of images assisting communication.

INTRODUCTION

Speech and language impairment is defined as a communication disorder that adversely affects not only a child's but also an adult's ability to talk, understand, read, and write. Augmentative and Alternative Communication (AAC) methods include all forms of communication (other than oral speech) that are used to express thoughts, needs, wants, and ideas. AAC devices can range from a simple picture board to a computer program that synthesizes speech from text. Generally, AAC systems are used when the communication involves facial expressions or gestures using symbols or pictures. People with severe speech or language problems rely on AAC to supplement existing speech or to replace non-functional speech. Special augmentative aids, such as picture and symbol communication boards and electronic devices, are available to help people express themselves. These can help to increase social interaction, school performance, and feelings of self-worth. AAC users should not stop using speech if they are able to do so. The AAC aids and devices are meant to enhance users' communication. AAC users encounter difficulty communicating via speech due to congenital and/or acquired disabilities occurring at any time across their lifespan. These conditions include but are not limited to autism, cerebral palsy, dual sensory impairments, genetic syndromes, intellectual and multiple disabilities, hearing impairment, diseases, strokes, and head injuries like aphasia.

AAC systems may help users to communicate by providing audio or visual prompts that support the user in speaking a word or phrase, or via synthesized speech (1). Many electronic AAC systems permit a user to pre-define words and phrases that would be difficult for the user to produce instantly.

Usually, electronic AAC systems have a high initial setup cost because of the specialized hardware or software required. However, the growing ubiquity of recent mobile devices and applications has led to widespread adoption of AAC software on typical mobile devices, tablets, and PCs (2).

Common smartphone hardware often includes capabilities beyond traditional AAC hardware, such as network connectivity and embedded sensors.

The capabilities of modern mobile devices provide an opportunity to improve the usability of AAC through context-aware computing (3). Current AAC solutions often expect the user to navigate through a hierarchical menu of speech and image options in order to speak or select an image. A networked, sensor-enabled AAC mobile device may be able to identify the user's current location, task, or conversational partner, and highlight conversational options that are most relevant to the user's current context. This could support ordering lunch when the user is in a restaurant, or discussing tennis with a sports fan. In this paper, we describe the design and development of a location-based Android application for assisting communication.

RELATED WORKS

Technology is often used to manage language disorders. Modern mobile devices such as smartphones offer various types of applications to facilitate communication, allowing users to maintain their independence and avoid social exclusion; these two principal features identify supportive technologies (4). McGrenere et al. (5) evaluated prototypes of aphasia-aware software for mobile devices. Participants reported that they could not read long streams of text like those found in recipes. As a result, the authors developed a recipe-book application, which replaced recipe text with pictures, and a planner (6), which noted each calendar event with pictures of the place and related people.

AphasiaWeb is in some sense an Augmentative and Alternative Communication (AAC) system, which guides users through a conversation using audio and visual prompts (7). Beukelman and Mirenda (8) give a comprehensive description of AAC systems. Kane et al. (9) describe an AAC system specific to aphasia. Their TalkAbout system runs on a mobile device and provides context-aware prompting. For example, in a café, a device's screen will automatically present the user words related to ordering coffee. This system provides audio and visual cues that guide the user through a conversation.

Daemen et al. (10) describe a system for telling stories through pictures, sounds, emotion icons, and written annotations. Each participant in the study responded differently to the software, revealing the difficulty in intrinsically designing a comprehensive system to manage aphasia. For instance, one participant valued sound as the most important input method, while another favored pictures.

Many other mobile AAC systems have been developed by Waller et al. (11), Allen et al. (12), Ahlsen et al. (13), Van Dijk et al. (14) and Keskinen et al. (15). The main contribution of our research paper is to present a system to help those with language disorders in an easy-to-use manner. Our application supports a wide range of users, such as those dealing with aphasia or autism and children. The desired result is that participants can easily communicate with other conversational partners through our application.

OUR STUDY

In essence, our system contains various categories of images. We combine some other important services to improve communication, such as Text to Speech (TTS) service, database, *Global Positioning System (GPS), and Internet access.*

First, this system searches through the available categories based on the current location given by the GPS. Each category contains various symbols, which are stored in the smartphone database. Then, the categories found near the current location are highlighted. A Text to Speech (TTS) service is an important part of any AAC system, and most current smartphones include this service. Thus, our proposed system also uses the TTS service to provide audio corresponding to the stored symbol. The overall system architecture is shown in Figure 1.

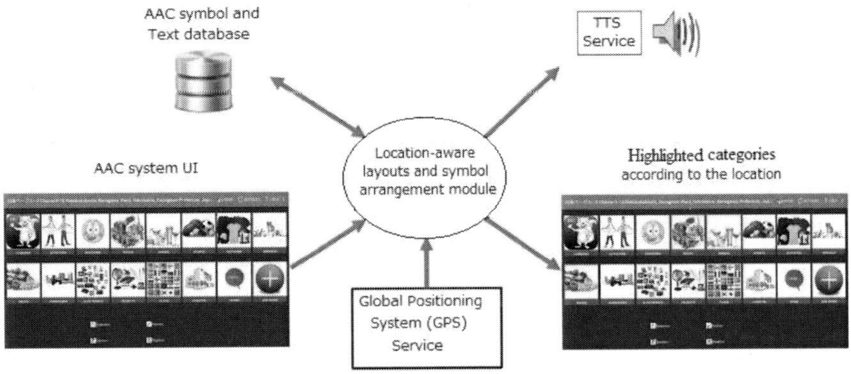

Figure 1. Architecture of the proposed Location-aware AAC system.

Hardware and software

The proposed system was developed on a latest Android-based tablet device. However, the application can also be installed on any Android-based smartphone using API level 8 or higher. Our prototype was tested on Sony Z4 tablet. This Android application was developed in Eclipse IDE and the application logic was written in Java. User data such as images and phrases were stored in the smartphone memory. We used the Google Location API and Google Place API to identify the location of the user. Finally, we used the default system Gmail client to send messages to other users.

User interface design

The purpose of our system is to provide users the ability to store, organize, browse, and speak stored words and phrases in addition to sending messages based on images. The current prototype enables users to browse items, add new items, and filter items based on the current location.

Browsing items: Each item in our system contains a picture and an associated word or phrase. The application is also capable of playing audio associated with the text using the built-in speech synthesizer. The context bar displays the current user location. Like other AAC systems, words and phrases may be assigned to hierarchical groups, which enable users to organize words and phrases by the location at which they are spoken or by the partner they most often have discussions with.

Adding new items: This process is similar to how users add content to existing AAC systems. Users may add new words or phrases to the system catalogue themselves. Adding a new item requires the user to: 1) input the text to be spoken; and 2) add an associated image. Words and phrases may be entered using the smartphone keyboard. The associated image may be captured by the user via the phone camera, selected from a set of previously captured images, or chosen automatically.

Filtering and updating items: The image categories are highlighted depending on the current location. The user is capable of updating the previously stored words or phrases.

This system provides the ability to detect the user's current location via GPS. It detects the user's location using the Google Location API, which relies upon GPS and Wi-Fi localization.

Flow diagram of the system

The basic flow diagram of our system is shown in Figure 2. The system algorithms are shown in Figure 3 as Algorithm 1 and Algorithm 2. Algorithm 1 contains the main method LocationAware AAC() and Algorithm 2 contains the supporting method GetCurrentLocation() for the main method. The method LocationAware AAC() calls the method GetCurrentLocation() to get the current location information using the Google Location API and Google Place API.

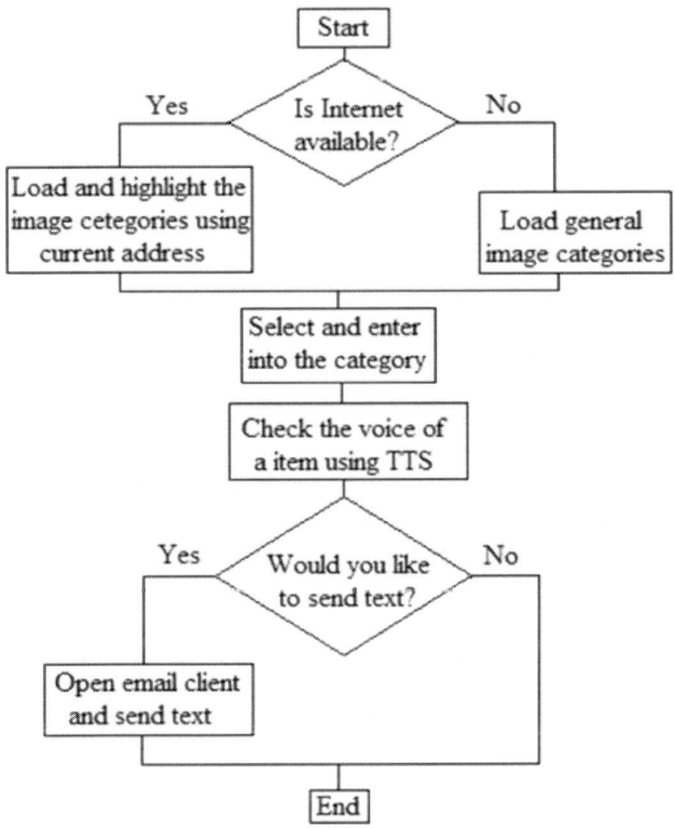

Figure 2. Flow diagram of the proposed system.

Detecting location

One of the unique features of mobile applications is location awareness. Mobile users take their devices with them everywhere; adding location awareness to our application offers users an enriched contextual experience. The location APIs available from Google Play Services facilitate the addition of location awareness to our application with automated location tracking. To detect the current location, we use the Google Location API. First, we need to check if Internet is accessible on the device. If Internet connection is available, then we find the current location using the Google

Place API. The Google Place API works with a specific category of word, such as food, bank, restaurant, school, etc. Then we apply a database query to match the current location with the stored image database. After results are found, categories that match with the current location are highlighted. Our current system checks categories within a 500 m radius from the current device position.

Text to Speech service

Our system was developed on Android OS (Version 6.0 Marshmallow) and allows us to convert text into voice, image into text, and also text to voice in a variety of languages. Java provides us the TextToSpeech class for this purpose. After choosing specific category, we can choose an image, at which point the application provides the word or full sentence that is stored in the image database.

Algorithm 1 Location-aware AAC application

```
procedure LocationAwareAAC()
    Get current location using GetCurrentLocation()
    ResultOfCategories = QueryResult using the current location.
    If(ResultCategories! = NULL) then load and highlight the categories. Otherwise no need
  to highlight and load categories.
    Select any category.
    Select any item to hear a full sentence using TTS.
    If the user wants to send an email, then send the text associated with the image to the
  partner. When the user sends the image it will automatically attach the current address.
    End
end procedure
```

Algorithm 2 Identify and return the current location

```
procedure GetCurrentLocation ()
    Check the Internet connection
    Find the current location using the Google Location API and Google Place API.
    Return location
end procedure
```

Figure 3. Algorithms of the proposed system.

Sending email

To send an email from our application, we can use the existing default email client provided by the smartphone OS such as Gmail, Outlook, K-9 Mail, etc. To achieve this, it was necessary to write an Activity that launches an email client, using an implicit Intent with the correct action and data. After choosing an image from a category, the system sends the text associated with that image using our device's default email client. When a healthy user receives the email, they are unaware of the sender's disability. In this way, our system improves empathy for the affected people.

OUR FINDINGS

The operation of our system is very simple, and is shown in Figure 4. Figures 4 (a) and (b) show the general categories and highlighted categories. If a restaurant, café, or supermarket is near the current location, the system will automatically highlight food, drink, and fruit categories. The last two images (c) and (d) of Figure 4 show the application after selecting the food category. Figure 4 (d) shows the message in the message box after confirming an item in the category. Finally, it is possible to send a message via email with the current location by pressing the send button.

This application is designed as a single user system to be used in everyday life for a person with limited or no speech capabilities. We have built the application with four distinct user communities in mind.

Aphasia users: This community can understand everything but have lost their ability to speak and possibly read. Therefore, they need icons to identify words and a high-level vocabulary.

Autism users: These users are characterized by difficulties in communicating and forming relationships with other people and in using language and understanding abstract concepts.

Children: If children wish to communicate with others when they are incapable of writing a sentence, this system can help them use images and voice to create a sentence.

Foreign language speakers: This system not only supports English but also other languages. Thus, users are able to easily operate, generate, and use the local language.

a) General categories

b) Highlighted categories

Figure 4. (Continued)

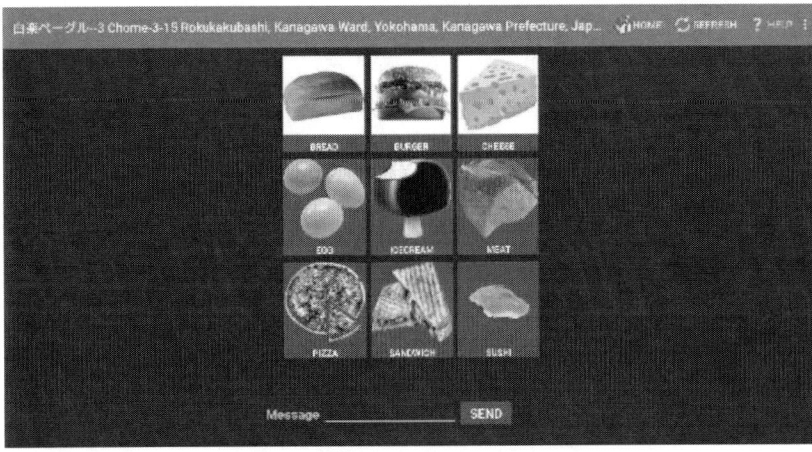

c) Category of Foods

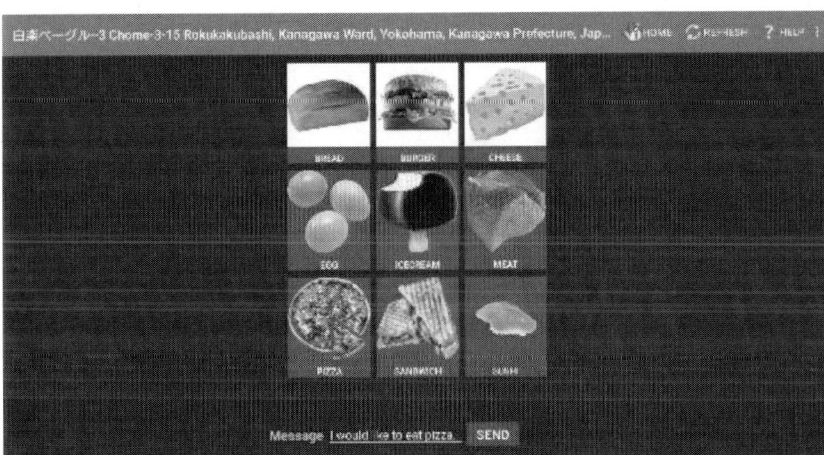

d) Message box with message after selecting the item pizza

Figure 4. Screenshot of the proposed system.

Usability testing is a method of testing a product while considering the target users in order to find usability problems existing in the product. A usability study aids in the removal of design issues, which should improve the product's end user experience. In usability testing, users are given tasks to perform while using the product and are observed to detect if they have any issue performing the tasks. While the user is performing a task, the usability team observes how the user is navigating the application as well as the user facial expression revealing how they react to the application. Depending on the observations, the usability team will suggest designing solutions. The application should be tested by real users because they tend to ignore the internal details of the system. Thus, we test our system on Japanese students in an English environment. After using our system, they rated it on a 5-point scale (1 = low, 5 = high). The result of their rating is shown in Table 1.

Table 1. Usability testing result

Participant	Age	Liked application	Better than current	Would use
P1	23	5	5	5
P2	23	4	5	5
P3	24	3	4	4
P4	23	5	5	4
P5	25	4	5	5

DISCUSSION

This paper demonstrates some communication methods that help individuals who struggle to produce or comprehend spoken or written language. The developed system provides mobile-based language therapy that can lead to positive changes in the language and functional communication skills of individuals suffering from speech and language disorders. This system can easily capture and manage pictures using a mobile device, which is useful to people with such disabilities. Users may find different applications for the system influenced not only by the nature of their diseases but also by their personal circumstances and communicative goals. For example, individuals with autism think in a visual way and recall visual images and memories easily. They can understand and benefit from concrete and visual information regarding daily events. Our system can present language in a consistent and visual manner. Children with autism, cerebral palsy, developmental disabilities, or rare genetic syndromes can receive communication and learning support through our system. We also believe our system can assist those who cannot speak foreign languages for successfully living in a foreign country.

Table 2 shows a comparison to other systems. The proposed system provides support for different types of users who have Android-based smartphones. AphasiaWeb is a web application that provides only visual and audio prompts for an aphasia user. It is a social networking web application where users can share their thoughts and feelings. Similarly, TalkAbout and PhotoTalk support only people with aphasia. However, our system is able to assist multiple user communities while supporting multiple languages. It can help users sending generated messages to other users similar to an instant messaging system. The proposed system takes in account mobile device GPS in order to use the current user location. This system has a rich image library that can properly support the user. Moreover, actual AAC systems are expensive and specialized. However, our system is implemented on an Android operating system, which is popular all over the world. When reading email messages, it is not possible to notice that the users have language impairment. Thus, they are treated as a normal user. As a result, our system automatically increases empathy towards the user.

Table 2. Comparison with other systems

Name	Platform	Type	Users
AphasiaWeb	Web	AAC for Social Networking	Aphasia
TalkAbout	iOS	AAC only	Aphasia
PhotoTalk	iPAQ pocket pc (windows)	AAC Only	Aphasia
Proposed system	Android	Instant messaging with AAC	Aphasia, autism, children, people with other languages

CONCLUSION

We have implemented an AAC system for people with speech disabilities. Most people with speech disabilities currently use AAC devices and mobile applications. At this time, available applications are more cost effective but less user-friendly and have limited vocabularies geared toward users with limited cognitive abilities and only available in English. In contrast, our system is user-friendly, contains a large vocabulary, targets users with higher cognitive abilities, supports multi-language use and location-awareness, and is extremely inexpensive. Finally, the first prototype was built on the latest Android OS because it has the largest user community all over the world. In addition, we have checked our system with occupational therapists. During the testing session, we received some suggestions. In the future, we intend to include their suggestions in our system to improve our goal to help individuals with language and speech related disabilities.

REFERENCES

[1] Beukelman DR, Mirenda P. Augmentative and alternative communication: Supporting children and adults with complex communication seeds. Baltimore, MD: Paul H Brookes, 2006.

[2] Vance A. Insurers fight speech-impairment remedy. New York Times 2009 Sep 14.

[3] Schilit B, Adams N, Want R. Context-aware computing applications. WMCSA'94 Proceedings of the 1994 First Workshop on Mobile Computing Systems and Applications; 1994 Dec 08, Washington, IEEE Computer Society Washington, DC, 1994:85-90.

[4] Newell AF, Carmichael A, Gregor P, Alm N. Information technology for cognitive support. The human-computer interaction handbook. Hillsdale, NJ: Erlbaum, 2003:464–481.

[5] McGrenere J, Davies R, Findlater L, Graf P, Klawe M, Moffatt K, et. al. Insights from the aphasia project: designing technology for and with people who have aphasia. CUU '03 Proceedings of the 2003 conference on Universal usability, 2003 Nov 10, New York, ACM New York, 2003:112–8.

[6] Moffatt K, McGrenere J, Purves B, Klawe M. The participatory design of a sound and image enhanced daily planner for people with aphasia. CHI '04 Proceedings of the SIGCHI Conference on Human Factors in Computing Systems, 2004 Apr 25, ACM New York, 2004:407–14.

[7] Hannah M and Chris J. AphasiaWeb: A social network for individuals with aphasia. ASSETS '13 Proceedings of the 15th International ACM SIGACCESS Conference on Computers and Accessibility, 2013 Oct 21; New York, ACM New York, 2013:4.

[8] Beukelman D, Mirenda P. Augmentative and alternative communication. Baltimore, MD: Paul H Brookes, 2005.

[9] Kane SK, Linam-Church B, Althoff K, McCall D. What we talk about: designing a context-aware communication tool for people with aphasia. ASSETS'12 Proceedings of the 14th international ACM SIGACCESS conference on Computers and accessibility, 2012 Oct 22, ACM New York, 2012:49–56.

[10] Daemen E, Dadlani P, Du J, Li Y, Erik-Paker P, Martens JB, et al. Designing a free style, indirect, and interactive storytelling application for people with aphasia. INTERACT'07 Proceedings of the 11th IFIP TC 13 international conference on Human-computer interaction, 2007 Nov 01. Berlin: Springer, 2007:221-34.

[11] Waller A, Dennis F, Brodie J, Cairns AY. Evaluating the use of TalksBac, a predictive communication device for nonfluent adults with aphasia. Int J Language Commun Disord 1998;33(1),45–70.

[12] Allen M, McGrenere J, Purves B. The design and field evaluation of PhotoTalk: a digital image communication application for people. Assets '07 Proceedings of the 9th international ACM SIGACCESS conference on Computers and accessibility, 2007 Oct 15, ACM New York, 2007:187-94.

[13] Ahlsen E, Geroimenko V. Virtual reality as a communication aid for persons with aphasia. The Second European Conference on Disability, Virtual Reality and Associated Technologies, 1998 Sep 10-11, Sweden, ECDVRAT and University of Reading, United Kingdom, 1998:229–35.

[14] Van BD, Dadlani P, Van HA, Biemans M. Life changes, connection stays: photo sharing and social connectedness for people with special needs. In: 28th Annual European Conference on Cognitive Ergonomics, 2010 Aug 25-27, Netherlands, ACM, 2010:135–42.

[15] Keskinen T, Heimonen T, Turunen M, Rajaniemi JP, Kauppinen S. Symbolchat: A flexible picture-based communication platform for users with intellectual disabilities. Interact Comput 2012;24(5),374-86.

In: Rehabilitation
Editors: Wendy Powell et al.
ISBN: 978-1-53612-080-6

Chapter 11

DIFFERENTIAL EFFECT OF NEUTRAL AND FEAR-STIMULUS VIRTUAL REALITY EXPOSURE ON PHYSIOLOGICAL INDICATORS OF ANXIETY IN ACROPHOBIA

Vaughan Powell*[*], *PhD, MA, BSc(Hons),
Wendy A Powell, PhD, BSc(Hons), BA, DC and
Patryk Maron, BSc(Hons)
School of Creative Technologies, University of Portsmouth,
Portsmouth, UK

This chapter presents a study which explores the physiological and behavioural indicators of anxiety during exposure to a virtual reality environment. Using 10 participants (five with acrophobia and five control) the study aimed to determine whether an increase in heart rate (HR) from baseline to VR (virtual reality) exposure is a sufficient measure for effectiveness of a virtual reality exposure therapy (VRET) stimulus, or whether there is a mediating effect of neutral VR exposure which should

[*] Corresponding author: Vaughan Powell, PhD, Senior Lecturer, School of Creative Technologies, University of Portsmouth, Winston Churchill Avenue, Portsmouth, United Kingdom. Email: vaughan.powell@port.ac.uk.

be taken into account. The participants all explored an immersive cityscape at ground level and at height, and both subjective and objective measures of physiological arousal were recorded. It was found that the VRET was successful in inducing an anxiety response in the participants with acrophobia, and moreover demonstrated that an increase in HR from baseline to VRET on its own should not be considered a reliable indicator of VRET efficacy, but that there should be an adjustment for the effect of neutral VR exposure on physiological arousal.

INTRODUCTION

Irrational or excessive fear or anxiety is a common problem, with an estimated 40% of the general population suffering from one or more fears of a specific object or situation in the course of their lifetime, with around 10% developing a specific phobia (1). Whilst some of these may be the direct result of a traumatic or harmful experience, many others are acquired through transmitted information or observation learning (2). This can make them challenging to treat, as it is often not just a simple case of addressing the underlying causative incident, but modifying the underlying pathological fear structures (3).

One of the most common forms of treatment for this type of therapy is gradual controlled exposure to the feared stimulus ("exposure therapy"). Hofmann (4) reports that exposure therapy involves a cognitive process of the extinction of fear by the absence of harm during exposure, and is at least as effective as the more complex cognitive therapy. Emotional processing theory (5) suggests that exposure therapy may work by breaking the stimulus-fear-avoidance cycle, producing new networks by exposing the individual to the feared stimulus without harm. Indeed, even imagined exposure to the feared consequence strengthens the discrimination between "thoughts about harm" and "real harm" (3). It is this ability of "imagined exposure" which is of particular interest, as it allows for the possibility of creating controlled virtual environment to support graded exposure.

This "virtual reality exposure therapy" (VRET) is being increasingly used to treat a variety of phobias and anxiety disorders (6, 7, 8), and has been demonstrated to be effective in reducing symptoms *in vivo* as well as in VR

(9, 10). However, the outcomes are not always consistent, and this may be due to a number of factors, including the individual patient (11, 12), the study protocol (10, 13) or the virtual environment itself (14, 15).

This paper is concerned with the last of these factors, the virtual environment, and the influence this may have on the efficacy of the VRET and hence on the treatment outcomes.

Background

Exposure therapy is a neural reconditioning process, which presents the feared stimulus in the absence of harm, undermining the negative associations and creating a new cognitive network (5). It is plausible that even exposure to virtual stimuli may support this cognitive reconditioning process, and indeed this hypothesis is supported by a number of reviews studying VRET outcomes (9, 10, 11, 16). However, studies vary in the reported efficacy of the VRET, and this may in part be due to the ability of the virtual environment (VE) to provide a suitable stimulus for effective exposure therapy.

Owens and Beidel suggest that effective VRET must meet three conditions in order to be consistent with the principles of emotional processing theory. Firstly, the exposure in the VE must be able to be generalised to real-life, secondly, the patient must feel present in the VR, and finally the VE should elicit physiological arousal (13). To a certain extent, the first condition can be met by careful design of the VRET application. The second and third are closely associated, as a VE is unlikely to elicit physiological arousal without a sense of presence in the exposure to a virtual fear stimulus, and both behavioural observation and physiological measurement are considered valid measures of presence (17). Thus in order to evaluate the potential efficacy of a VRET application, we can use either behavioural observations or physiological indicators, as well as more traditional measures of presence.

Previous studies have shown that VRET can elicit physiological arousal (8, 13), but this has not generally been correlated to observable behaviour changes or subjective distress. For example, a study which compared reported presence to physiological observations used only a general presence questionnaire, and did not include any behavioural observations (18). When evaluating such studies, it is difficult to be certain whether the increased physiological arousal can be attributed to a fear stimulus, or to some other factor of the virtual environment. In addition, it is not certain whether exposure to virtual reality can itself trigger physiological arousal, even in the absence of fear or distress.

Slater and colleagues (8) demonstrated a significant difference in heart rate (HR) between speaking in an empty virtual room and speaking to a virtual audience, confirming that HR within a virtual environment is dependent on the level of stimulus. However, in the absence of baseline (non-VR) HR data, the level of elevation of HR which would indicate successful fear-arousal is unclear. It has been suggested that an increase in HR >15 bpm is indicative of sufficient immersion for exposure therapy (19), but again this study did not examine the change in HR from non-VR to baseline VR, and so could not differentiate between rise in HR due to the fear-inducing stimulus from that induced solely by exposure to VR.

We suggest that in order to evaluate whether a virtual environment meets the conditions necessary for VRET, it is necessary to demonstrate that the fear stimulus has a differential effect on physiological arousal beyond that which may be induced by baseline VR exposure. In this preliminary study we expose both an acrophobic group and a control group to an immersive VR environment followed by a virtual height stimulus. We hypothesise that there will be an increase in HR on exposure to VR, even in the absence of a fear stimulus, and that there will be a further increase in HR when participants are exposed to the virtual height. Further, we hypothesise that there will be a differential change in HR between phobic and non-phobic participants when exposed to height, but not in the other conditions. Finally, we hypothesise that there will be correlations between observed behaviour, reported anxiety and HR in the VR exposure.

Table 1. Participant demographics

Participant	**01**	**02**	**03**	**04**	**05**	**06**	**07**	**08**	**09**	**10**
Acrophobia	None	None	Mild	Mild	Mild	None	None	Moderate	Moderate	None
Age	21	22	24	20	26	19	21	21	21	21
Gender	m	m	m	m	m	m	m	f	f	m

OUR STUDY

The study was a mixed 3x2 factorial design, with one within-subjects factor (VR condition), and one between-subjects factor (acrophobia).

The VR exposure and the acrophobia tendency were the independent variables, and heart rate (HR) was the primary dependent variable. In addition, presence, subjective fear and behavioural observations were recorded.

Participants

Ten participants were recruited from the School of Creative Technologies. There were 8 males and 2 females, aged from 19-26 (mean age 22). Five participants reported mild or moderate acrophobia, and five reported no fear of heights.

Measures

On arrival, participants were asked for a self-rating of their fear of heights. This was coded as none = 0, mild = 1 and moderate = 2. Heart rate data was recorded continuously via a Polar H7 monitor during the pre-exposure, VR-neutral exposure and VR-height phases of the study.

Behavioural observations were made throughout the interaction with the virtual environment. Behaviours were coded from 0 (no signs of anxiety) to 5 (signs of severe anxiety).

A post-test short questionnaire (20) evaluated the sense of presence during the VR exposure, and participants were also asked to rate their subjective sense of fear during the exposure on a scale of 1-10.

Experimental setup

As previously discussed, it is important to induce a sense of presence ("being there") for effective VRET. In order to evaluate the differential effect of VR stimuli on HR, we need to use a virtual environment which is optimised to support the induction of presence. Since the visual quality of the environment and the level of interaction available to the user are both important factors in inducing a sense of presence (21), we designed a realistic virtual cityscape and used full body motion capture to support fully immersive interaction.

For the virtual environment to run smoothly during the VR exposure several optimisations had to be made, one of which was combination of low and high polygon 3D assets to ensure that frame rates do not drop below comfort zone of around 75fps. A technique known as *Level of Details* (LODs) was used to dynamically adjust the detail of meshes in the virtual environment depending how close the participant is to the object. The further away the object, the lower the detail it will have and closer you get towards it the sharper the textures and more polygons will be visible resulting in greater overall performance and more pleasant experience.

A 3D model of a cityscape was created in Autodesk 3DS Max and then deployed in Unreal Engine 4. Physical based rendering (PBR) was used in order to create realistic lighting effects. A walkway between two buildings was constructed on the 5th floor, and this was made of a combination of concrete and glass textures. Finally, there was a lookout point on the roof of a seven-story building (see Figure 1).

Figure 1. From left to right: Cityscape, concrete and glass walkway and roof lookout point.

The participants' motion was captured using Vicon T10 cameras and a full-body motion capture suit with 59 markers. A PC was used which was capable of running the motion capture and application in real time at a minimum frame rate of 120fps. Between the Motion Capture hardware and Unreal Engine 4 it was essential to have a solution which streamed the data captured from the body motion, and translate it to a rigged animation in real time. For this we used Vicon's Pegasus retargeting software. This allows us to bridge both technologies seamlessly and result in highly responsive real-time full body control in the virtual environment.

Participants viewed the virtual environment using the Oculus Rift DK2, and their movements were mapped directly onto a self-avatar, with real-time rendering of shadows.

Procedure

Participants were briefed on the study and signed an informed consent sheet. They were also reminded that they could stop the study at any point if they felt uncomfortable or overly anxious. They were then fitted with the Polar H7 monitor on a chest strap, and then donned a motion capture suit. Fifty-nine optical markers were applied at predefined anatomical landmarks (see Figure 2), and a calibration sequence of movements was performed. During this time (3-5 minutes) a baseline HR was recorded.

The participants were then fitted with the head mounted display and were able explore the cityscape at ground level. They were given a few minutes to acclimatise to the VR environment and the VR-baseline heart rate was recorded during this time.

Finally, the participants were asked to close their eyes for 10 seconds while they were moved to the elevated areas of the virtual environment. They were given a number of tasks, including stepping onto the bridge, crossing over a glass area, and leaning over the rooftop to look down to the street, which accumulated around 10 to 15 minutes for each participant's total exposure. Again, HR was recorded during this VR-height exposure.

Figure 2. The motion capture suit with optical markers.

After the completion of the tasks at height (or sooner if the participants requested "escape" from the scenario), the participant completed a questionnaire with 3 questions to score the sense of presence, a Likert score for the level of fear experienced, and a free-text question regarding aspects of the experience which interfered with the sense of presence.

FINDINGS

A repeated measures ANOVA was conducted to compare the effect of no-VR, VR, and VR-height exposure on heart rate (HR). There was a significant effect of VR condition on the mean HR [$F(2,18) = 87.54$, $p = .000$.].

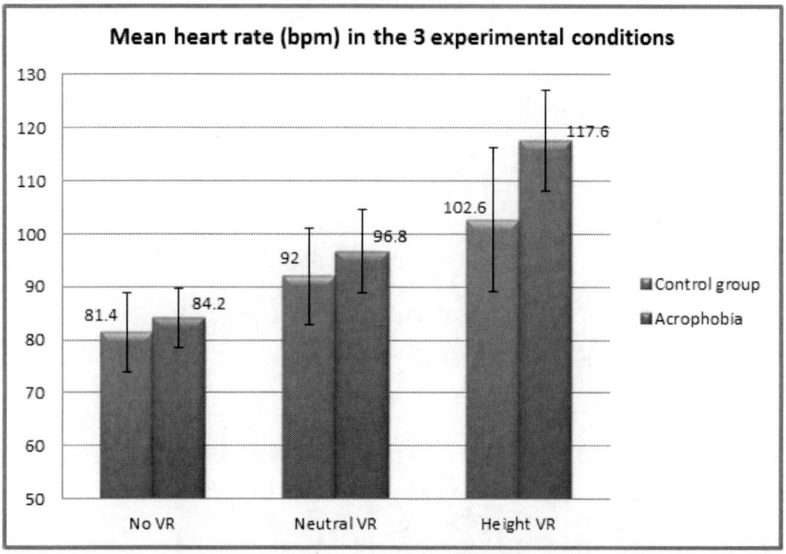

Figure 3. The differential effect of non-VR, neutral VR and VR-height on heart rate.

Post hoc comparison demonstrated that HR was significantly lower in no-VR than VR [$t(9) = 10.57$, $p = 0.00$.], lower in no-VR than VR-height [$t(9) = 5.51$, $p = 0.00$.], and lower in VR than VR-height [$t(9) = 8.19$, $p = 0.00$.] (Figure 3).

Differential effect of acrophobia on HR during fear stimulus

There was a positive correlation between the level of acrophobia and the VR-height HR [$r = 0.679$, $n = 10$, $p < 0.05$]. There was no correlation between the level of acrophobia and the baseline HR or neutral-VR HR.

Correlation between behaviour, HR and reported anxiety during fear stimulus

There was no anxious behaviour observed while the participants explored the city street, and all the observed anxious behaviour occurred during exposure to the height stimuli. There was a positive correlation between the observed anxious behaviour and the reported level of fear [$r = .909$, $n = 10$, $p – 0.00$.], between the observed behaviour and the HR at height [$r = .655$, $n = 10$, $p < 0.05$], and between the reported level of fear and the HR at height [$r = .827$, $n = 10$, $p < 0.01$].

DISCUSSION

This study set out to explore the differential effect of neutral and fear-stimulus VR exposure on physiological indicators of anxiety. There was a significant increase in HR on exposure to neutral VR environments in both groups, with a mean rise of 12 bpm. This rise was not associated with any anxiety behaviour, and was not correlated to the level of acrophobia. Since the suggested indicator for successful immersion for exposure therapy is only 15 bpm, it would appear that we run the risk of a false positive evaluation of a VRET if we compare non-VR HR to exposure HR without adjusting for the direct effect of neutral VR exposure on HR.

The exposure to the VR height stimulus elicited a further significant rise in HR in all groups, but this time there was a significant correlation between reported acrophobia and the increased HR, with the mean increase in acrophobia being 19.4 bpm, compared to a rise of 10.6 bpm in the control group. Furthermore, all of the acrophobia group experienced a minimum rise of 15 bpm when moving from the neutral VR stimulus to the VR height stimulus. This suggests that the 15 bpm could indeed be a useful indicator of a successful exposure in a VRET environment *but only when it has been measured from a neutral VR* baseline. Indeed, when the increase in HR is compared directly to baseline, without adjusting for VR exposure, 80% of the control group (no acrophobia) exhibit a rise >15 bpm, without showing any sign of anxiety behaviour or reported fear.

This study is not without its limitations. The initial sample size is small, and does not have an equal gender balance between groups, additionally all participants do come from the School of Creative Technologies which is a clear limitation. Although this may not have influenced the results, a larger sample with a more homogenous demographic distribution is needed to confirm these initial findings. Furthermore, activity is known to influence HR, and although the participants were able to move around in all three conditions, it was not possible to completely control for any potential effect of movement on HR. A follow-up study with seated participants would help to identify any movement-artefacts in the recorded HR data. Finally, there were a number of incidents which caused a break in immersion, including “stepping off the edge”, hearing other voices in the motion capture room, and “retargeting errors” on the hands of the avatar. For a future study, the participants would be issued with noise-cancelling headphones, and a more robust smoothing algorithm used to maintain consistent movement of the avatar. Whilst there is a good correlation between observed behaviour scores and the respective self reporting of anxiety and the recorded heart rate, the behaviour coding was not a standardised coding system but was created bespoke for the project. The observational data was recorded by the author without prior knowledge of the behaviour coding. The coding of behaviour was then designed by a second member of the team and then applied to the observational data. This was then checked and found to be relatively consistent in its application and interpretation across the participants by a third member of the team. Such an approach, whilst mitigating bias, does have limitations and in future work a blind double coding approach will be applied from the outset. It has been suggested that passive haptics can significantly increase presence in VR (Meehan et al., 2002), and thus the use of a raised surface for the bridge, and a small platform for the roof would be used in future studies

In summary, this study is the first to indicate the need to adjust for the rise in HR in neutral VR before using HR increases as an indicator for successful VRET fear stimulus. It is important to elicit the physiological and behavioural responses of anxiety during exposure therapy in order to achieve successful extinction of fear during the therapeutic process (Owens & Beidel, 2014), and careful evaluation of the VRET stimulus environment before deployment should facilitate more consistent outcomes.

ACKNOWLEDGMENTS

With thanks to Alex, Joe and Scott for assisting with the motion capture and supporting the data collection for the study.

REFERENCES

[1] Van Houtem CMHH, Laine ML, Boomsma DI, Ligthart L, van Wijk AJ, De Jongh A. A review and meta-analysis of the heritability of specific phobia subtypes and corresponding fears. J Anxiety Disord 2013; 27(4): 379-88.

[2] Rachman S. The conditioning theory of fearacquisition: A critical examination. Behav Res Ther 1977; 15(5): 375-87.

[3] Foa EB, Huppert JD, Cahill SP. Emotional processing theory: An update pathological anxiety: Emotional processing in etiology and treatment. New York: Guilford, 2006: 3-24.

[4] Hofmann SG. Cognitive processes during fear acquisition and extinction in animals and humans: Implications for exposure therapy of anxiety disorders. Clin Psychol Rev 2008; 28(2): 199-210.

[5] Foa EB, Kozak MJ. Emotional processing of fear: exposure to corrective information. Psychol Bull 1986; 99(1): 20-35.

[6] Carlin AS, Hoffman HG, Weghorst S. Virtual reality and tactile augmentation in the treatment of spider phobia: a case report. Behav Res Ther 1997; 35(2): 153-8.

[7] Emmelkamp PMG, Krijn M, Hulsbosch AM, de Vries S, Schuemie MJ, van der Mast CAPG. Virtual reality treatment versus exposure *in vivo*: a comparative evaluation in acrophobia. Behav Res Ther 2002; 40(5): 509-16.

[8] Slater M, Pertaub DP, Barker C, Clark DM. An experimental study on fear of public speaking using a virtual environment. Cyberpsychol Behav 2006; 9(5): 627-33.

[9] Coelho CM, Waters AM, Hine TJ, Wallis G. The use of virtual reality in acrophobia research and treatment. J Anxiety Disord 2009; 23(5): 563-74.

[10] Parsons TD, Rizzo AA. Affective outcomes of virtual reality exposure therapy for anxiety and specific phobias: A meta-analysis. J Behav Ther Exp Psychiatr 2008; 39(3): 250-61.

[11] Krijn M, Emmelkamp PMG, Olafsson RP, Biemond R. Virtual reality exposure therapy of anxiety disorders: A review. Clin Psychol Rev 2004; 24(3): 259-81.

[12] Wiederhold BK, Wiederhold MD. Lessons learned from 600 virtual reality sessions. Cyberpsychol Behav 2000; 3(3): 393-400.

[13] Owens ME, Beidel DC. Can Virtual Reality Effectively elicit distress associated with social anxiety disorder? J Psychopathol Behav Assess 2014; 37(2): 296-305.

[14] Miyahira SD, Folen RA, Stetz M, Rizzo A, Kawasaki MM. Use of immersive virtual reality for treating anger. Stud Health Technol Inform 2010; 154: 82-6.

[15] Slater M, Pertaub DP, Steed A. Public speaking in virtual reality: facing an audience of avatars. IEEE Computer Graphics and Applications 1999; 19(2): 6-9.

[16] Powers MB, Emmelkamp PMG. Virtual reality exposure therapy for anxiety disorders: A meta-analysis. J Anxiety Disord 2008; 22(3): 561-9.

[17] Lee KM. Presence explicated. Commun Theory 2004; 14(1): 27-50.

[18] Meehan M, Insko B, Whitton M, Frederick P, Brooks J. Physiological measures of presence in stressful virtual environments. ACM Trans Graph 2005; 21(3): 645-52.

[19] Walshe DG, Lewis EJ, Kim SI, O'Sullivan K, Wiederhold BK. Exploring the use of computer games and virtual reality in exposure therapy for fear of driving following a motor vehicle accident. Cyberpsychol Behav 2003; 6(3) 329-334.

[20] Slater M, Usoh M. Presence in immersive virtual environments. Paper presented at the Virtual Reality Annual International Symposium 1993 Sept 18-22.

[21] North MM, North SM. A comparative study of sense of presence of traditional virtual reality and immersive environments. Australasian J Inform Systems 2016; 20: 1-15.

In: Rehabilitation
Editors: Wendy Powell et al.
ISBN: 978-1-53612-080-6

Chapter 12

INTEGRATIVE VIRTUAL REALITY THERAPY PRODUCES LASTING BENEFITS FOR A YOUNG WOMAN SUFFERING FROM CHRONIC PAIN AND DEPRESSION POST CANCER SURGERY: A CASE STUDY

Gregory House*[1], *PhD, Grigore C Burdea*[1,*], *PhD, Namrata Grampurohit*[1], *PhD, Kevin Polistico*[1], *BS, Doru Roll*[1], *MS, Frank Damiani*[2], *MD, Jasdeep Hundal*[3], *PsyD and Didier Demesmin*[4], *MD

[1]Bright Cloud International Corp, Highland Park, New Jersey, US
[2]Roosevelt Care Center, Edison, New Jersey, US
[3]Hundal Neuropsychology Group, Watchung, New Jersey, US
[4]University Pain Medicine Center, Summerset, New Jersey, US

In this chapter we present a case study, which was part of an evaluation of the BrightArm Duo Rehabilitation System for treating the effects of

* Correspondence: Grigore C Burdea PhD, President, Bright Cloud International Corp, 29 L'Ambiance Court, Highland Park, NJ, United States. Email: president@brightcloudint.com.

chronic upper body pain following breast cancer surgery. The subject was a 22-year old woman with burning and stabbing pain in the right upper arm. Training consisted of playing custom bimanual 3D games while seated at a gravity-modulating robotic table. The therapy consisted of 16 sessions over eight weeks. Standardized assessments demonstrated a meaningful improvement in the motor, cognitive and emotive domains with a statistically significant reduction in pain. Gains transferred to daily activities enabling the subject to resume full time employment, driving and socializing.

INTRODUCTION

The psychological, social and behavioral impact of cancer at a young age can be tremendous (1). As the number of young cancer survivors increases, their quality of life after cancer treatment becomes an important concern (2). With improved detection and progress in management of breast cancer (3), the survivors need improved rehabilitation approaches to address and overcome the resulting complications from that treatment. Depression and chronic pain in shoulder and arm following breast cancer surgery are prevalent and can lead to life-long psychological, cognitive and physical impairments. It is important to have rehabilitation techniques that can produce long lasting benefits for women, while being gradated in difficulty, interactive and fun.

Virtual reality (VR) offers benefits for other diagnostic conditions and provides a new and unique opportunity in the rehabilitation of women with breast cancer. VR analgesia, pioneered by Hoffman (4) for burn wound care, has subsequently been used to reduce chemotherapy-related distress in women with breast cancer (5). Virtual reality has great potential for use in acute and chronic pain by providing a non-opioid 'virtual analgesic' response (6). Virtual reality therapy has been tried in breast cancer to alleviate symptoms during chemotherapy (5). However, to the authors' knowledge no clinical trials have been conducted to study VR effectiveness in breast cancer survivors with chronic upper body pain and related depression.

The BrightArm Duo Rehabilitation System (Bright Cloud International, New Jersey, USA) is an experimental robotic platform that modulates gravity loading on the upper extremities (UEs). The ability to unload gravity makes it appropriate for individuals with weak arms and diminished ability to grasp, such as those suffering from chronic UE pain. BrightArm Duo uses VR to engage the patient in upper body bimanual integrative exercises that provide motor and cognitive training and affective relief. This integrative virtual rehabilitation has been found to be beneficial in prior BrightArm Duo studies of elderly individuals with chronic stroke residing in skilled nursing facilities (7). These earlier studies have shown benefits to cognition and depression reduction, which in theory could benefit breast cancer survivors with the same type of impairments. Thus, a feasibility study was conducted (N=6) to explore the feasibility of BrightArm Duo Rehabilitation System for the treatment of chronic pain in breast cancer survivor post-surgery, and who also have depression and cognitive deficits. The case described here was the youngest subject participating in that study.

OUR STUDY

The BrightArm Duo Rehabilitation System consisted of a robotic rehabilitation table, two computerized forearm supports, a 27” monitor, a laptop computer for the therapist, a remote clinical server and a library of custom integrative rehabilitation games. The library of custom games was developed in Unity 3D (8) for uni-manual and bi-manual motor (shoulder, elbow, grasp), emotive (depression) and cognitive (executive function, focusing, short-term and delayed memory, working memory and task sequencing) training. The subject interacted with these serious games through active arm movement and power grasp, both being tracked in real time. The forearms of the subject were placed onto low-friction supports outfitted with two 770 nm LED towers and a rubber pear bulb connected to an internal differential pressure sensor. The hand position was determined with better than 0.5 mm accuracy. Subject’s grasp strength of the rubber pear was measured by the pressure sensor and communicated wirelessly to the laptop station at a data rate better than 40 packets per second. Each session, the system automatically adapted to the subject's forearm movement and grasp capabilities. Game difficulty, session duration, gravity unloading/ loading (gravity assistance/resistance during training) on her upper extremity, were all gradated over the length of the training (7). Tilting upwards provided resistance when moving away from the trunk. Conversely, tilting downwards assisted weak arm movement.

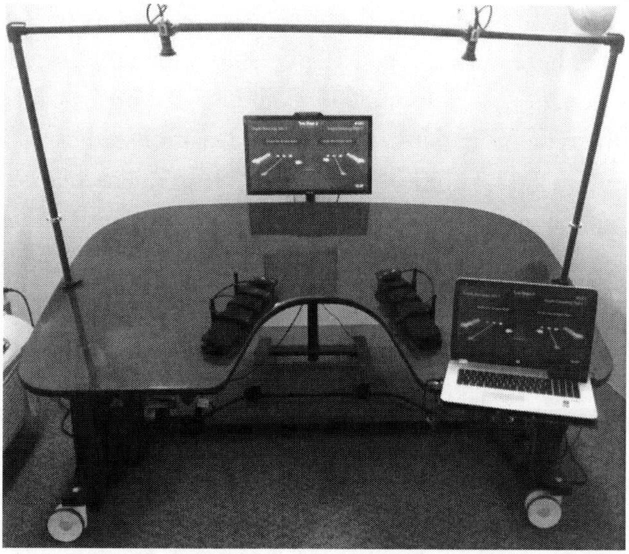

Figure 1. BrightArm Duo Table tilted upwards with two arm supports for user interaction and therapist laptop rendering Pick & Place game to the 27" monitor.

Figure 2 shows the screen images of the nine games used in the study. In *Breakout 3D,* the subject bounced a virtual ball toward an array of crates using paddle avatars. The game trained shoulder abduction/adduction or flexion/extension depending on the orientation of the crates, as well as focusing and executive function. The matching card games *Card Island* and *Remember that Card* trained short-term and delayed visual and auditory memory, grasp strength, shoulder abduction/adduction, and shoulder flexion/extension. For *Musical Drums,* the subject controlled drum stick avatars to strike a series of notes that drifted across (up to four) drums. This game trained focusing and motor control. The *Xylophone* game trained short-term auditory and visual memory by having the subject repeat a sequence of musical notes using mallet avatars. In *Pick & Place*, the subject grasped a ball from among multiple choices and then moved it to a fixed target of matching color, using shoulder flexion/extension or abduction/adduction arm movements. The game trained working memory and motor control as subject was asked to follow an ideal straight line to the target. Playing *Arm Slalom* induced shoulder rotations in order to guide a skier avatar through a downhill slalom course. In the *Avalanche* game, the subject controlled pickaxe and shovel avatars through grasp and arm movements. The task was to break and clear a series of ice walls so to free people trapped in a cottage. In *Treasure Hunt*, the subject used one or two shovel avatars to clear sand and uncover a series of buried treasures, before they were buried again by periodic sand storms.

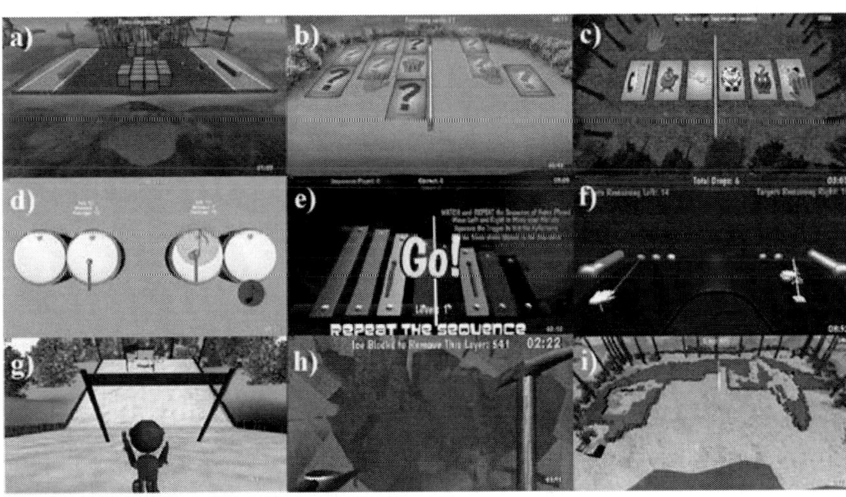

Figure 2. Nine game screen images: a) Breakout 3D; b) Card Island; c) Remember that Card; d) Musical Drums; e) Xylophone; f) Pick & Place; g) Arm Slalom;

h) Avalanche; i) Treasure Hunt. © Bright Cloud International Corp. Reprinted by permission.

Training protocol

The feasibility study followed a single subject A1-B1-A2-A3 design with training (B1) consisting of a total of 16 sessions, two sessions per week for 8 weeks. Standardized assessments of motor, cognitive and emotive state were performed pre-training (A1), post-training (A2) and at 8-week follow-up (A3). The training sessions progressed from 20 minutes to 50 minutes in duration, and the BrightArm Duo robotic table was tilted upwards progressively from a minimum of 0° (horizontal) at the start of the protocol to a maximum of 20° in the last training sessions. This corresponded to gravity unloading at the beginning of the therapy then progressively increased gravity loading as the subjects trained in later sessions. The Western Institutional Review Board, an independent board overseeing research involving human subjects, reviewed and approved the study protocol in accordance with Federal Guidelines. The subject was recruited at the University Pain Medicine Center (Somerset, NJ) and training took place at Roosevelt Care Center, a clinical facility in Edison, NJ in summer 2015. The subject received a $25 monetary compensation for each session attended however to the authors' knowledge this was not her primary reason for participation. The subject was genuinely interested in this experimental therapy to help manage her upper body pain symptoms.

CASE STORY

The subject was a 22-year old single woman of a mixed race, African American and White, with post-surgical chronic pain for the preceding 9 years. This chronic pain was localized to right upper arm and was burning, throbbing and stabbing in nature. She occasionally also reported pain in lower back, upper back, breast, hip and neck which was described as nagging. The subject reported that moving made her pain worse and nothing made it better. She had severe depression, difficulty socializing and had one suicidal attempt. As a consequence of her pain she kept her right arm in a sling which resulted in employment difficulties. She worked as a certified nursing assistant in home health care with hourly work that she would have to cancel many times due to pain. She was recruited from the University Pain Medicine Center where she followed up routinely with a pain medicine physician with a reported pain level of 6 to 8 on Numerical Pain Rating Scale (9) and not undergoing any physical or occupational therapy at the time of her enrollment in the experimental study. The surgical procedure on her breast reported when she was 13 years old did not have any medical records for verification of diagnosis. She underwent lumpectomy of her right breast again in 2008 and cyst removal from left breast in 2007. She reported taking Tromodol 50 mg and Percocet 10 mg at pre-training. She had tried multiple therapies in the past as indicated in her clinical notes. These ranged from pain medications, to physical therapy twice a week for 10 weeks from January to April 2014, to home exercises.

Data collection instruments

Therapy session data (B1) included supported arm reach baseline on the BrightArm Duo table (as measured by overhead digital cameras used in tracking), power grasp strength baseline (as measured by a forearm support grasp sensor), heart rate and blood pressure. In addition B1 data included the number of active movements and grasp repetitions for each arm during a session, as well as game performance data (score, errors, completion time) collected during play. Pain was assessed using the Numeric Pain Rating Scale (NRS) administered verbally by the attending OT. This pain measure has validity in measuring cancer-related pain intensity (9). Skin temperature was measured during the sessions with basis wristwatch that was worn on the subject's unaffected arm. Blood pressure and pulse were measured before and after each session using Omron 7 Series upper arm blood pressure monitor.

Occupational therapy evaluations were done pre-training, post-training and at eight week follow-up by a blinded Senior Occupational Therapist (OT) consultant who was not training the subject. This OT evaluation involved assessment of upper extremity function using the Fulg-Meyer

Assessment - Upper Extremity Section (FMA)(10), the Chedokee Arm and Hand Inventory – 9 (CAHAI-9)(11) for bimanual tasks and the Jebsen Hand Function Test (JHFT)(12) for hand function. Arm and hand range of motion were measured using mechanical goniometers, shoulder strength was assessed using wrist weights, grasp strength was measured with a Jamar mechanical dynamometer and a Jamar pinch meter. In addition the subject was assessed for her degree of independence in activities of daily living (ADL) involving the upper extremity, using the Upper Extremity Functional Index 20 (UEFI-20) (13).

Neuropsychological evaluations were done by a blinded research assistant under the supervision of a licensed clinical neuropsychologist pre-training, post-training and at follow-up. These were measures of depression severity, attention/concentration, processing speed, learning, memory, and executive function. The standardized measures used were the Beck Depression Inventory, Second Edition (BDI-II),(14) the Neuropsychological Assessment Battery Executive Functioning Module (Generation subtest) (15), the Hopkins Verbal Learning Test, Revised (HVLT-R) (16), the Brief Visuospatial Memory Test, Revised (BVMT-R) (17), the Trail Making Test A and B (TMT) (18). Alternate test forms were used whenever possible to minimize test-taking practice effects. Raw scores were utilized in all data analysis. Both evaluating clinicians were blinded to the therapy methodology and scope.

At the end of weeks 4 and 8 of VR training, the subject rated her experience on a custom paper-based subjective evaluation questionnaire with ten questions. The questions were: 1) “The system was easy to use?”; 2) “Playing games with my affected arm(s) was easy?”; 3) “I had no pain or discomfort in my upper body?”; 4)“Instructions given to me were useful?”; 5) “Playing games with both arms was easy?”; 6) “I was not bored while exercising?”; 7) “The length of the exercising in a day was appropriate?”; 8) “There were few technical problems?”; 9) “I would encourage others to used it?”; 10) “I liked the system overall?” Each question was rated on a 5-point Likert scale, from 1 meaning “strongly disagree” (least desirable outcome) to 5 meaning “strongly agree” (most desirable one). The subject could add free form comments on the evaluation form.

FINDINGS

The subject exercised a total of 20,130 active arm repetitions and 7,020 hand grasps. The BrightArm Duo tilt was gradually increased over the study span, from 0° initially to 20° upwards at the end. Figure 3a show active arm repetitions increased from about 320 in session 1 to over 1,500 repetitions in session 16 with peak activity around session 5 and 11. Hand grasps increased from 45 in session 1 to 971 by session 16. The intensity of play increased with session number as well. If session length is normalized to maximum duration of 51.2 minutes, arm movement and hand grasps would increase along a slope of 878 ($p=0.18$) and 1,011 ($p<0.001$) repetitions between session 1 and 16. The subject played a total of 412 games over a total of 567 minutes. The exercising duration steadily increased from 21.2 minutes/session at the start to 51.2 minutes/session at the end. Both game difficulty and subject performance increased over the study. Figure 3b illustrates how composite games scores increased from 43 (session 1) to 65 (session 16). The linear regression fit of the data points yielded a statistically significant trend line ($p<0.001$) corresponding to a 22 point increase in average game score from about 47 points in session 1 to about 69 points in session 16.

Pain and skin temperature outcomes

The subject's reported pain and skin temperature were captured every session. Figure 4a illustrates the reported maximum upper extremity pain on the 10 point Numerical Pain Rating Scale by session number. As seen by the statistically significant trend line ($p=0.01$), there was marked reduction in reported pain of 4.4 points over the course of the study. The increase in reported pain towards the end of the experimental therapy coincided with the subject stopping taking her pain medication. Figure 4b plots the average skin temperature by session number as measured at the wrist of the subject's unaffected arm. The linear regression fit of the data points yielded a statistically significant trend line (p=0.001) corresponding to a 10.25°F increase in skin temperature over the 16 sessions. This is indicative of increased blood flow to the upper extremities in response to increased use of the affected arm.

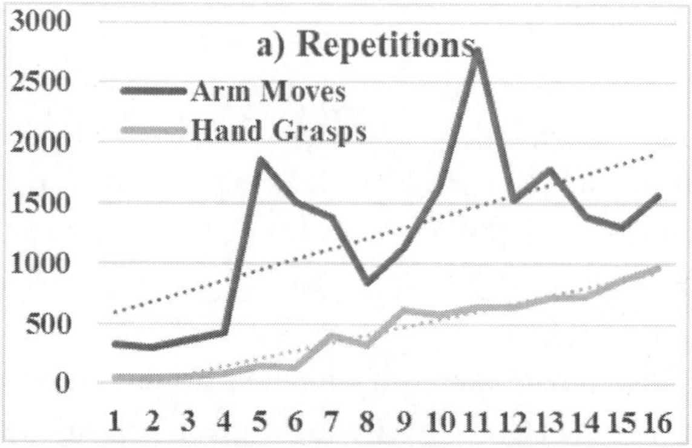

a

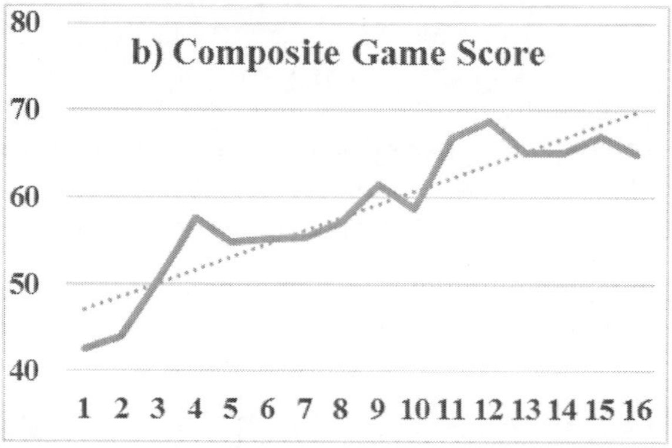

b

Figure 3. a) Arm and hand repetitions and b) composite game score by session number for the cancer survivor experiencing post-surgery chronic pain. © Bright Cloud International Corp. Reprinted by permission.

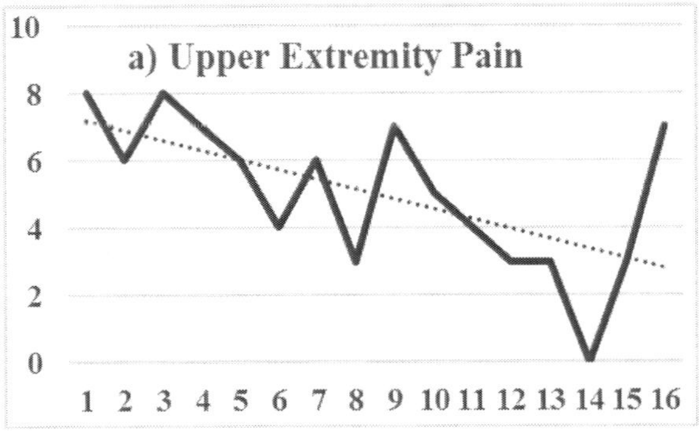

a

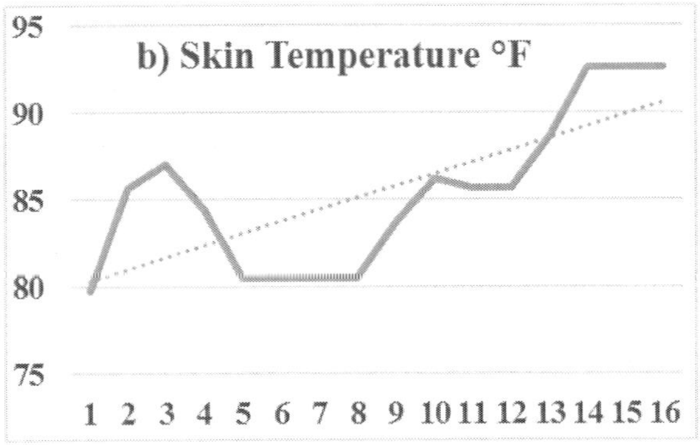

b

Figure 4. a) Maximum upper extremity pain and b) affected arm skin temperature by session for the cancer survivor experiencing post-surgery chronic pain. © Bright Cloud International Corp. Reprinted by permission.

Upper Extremity Active Range of Motion

The subject's range of motion was evaluated for the affected and unaffected arms at pre-training (A1), post-training (A2) and follow-up (A3). The elbow and finger values were within normal limits. In Table 1, 10 of 12 range of motion measures improved at A2 and A3 relative to A1. The affected arm maintained substantial gains at A3: Abduction (111°), Flexion (89°), Adduction (40°), External Rotation (31°), and Extension (19°). The unaffected arm improvements were more modest at A3: Flexion (16°), Abduction (10°), Extension (9°) with Internal Rotation moderately decreasing (20°). The minimal clinically important difference (MCID) is 8° for shoulder range of motion improvement (19).

Table 1. Shoulder range of motion (degrees) for the post-surgery cancer survivor experiencing chronic pain. © Bright Cloud International Corp. Reprinted by permission

	Affected Shoulder					Unaffected Shoulder				
Variable	A1	A2	A3	A2-A1	A3-A1	A1	A2	A3	A2-A1	A3-A1
Flexion	58	150	147	+ 92	+ 89	132	146	148	+ 14	+ 16
Extension	23	73	42	+ 50	+ 19	58	77	67	+ 19	+ 9
Abduction	27	157	138	+ 130	+ 111	140	148	150	+ 8	+ 10
Adduction	0	56	40	+ 56	+ 40	33	50	40	+ 17	+ 7
Internal rot.	38	55	40	+ 17	+ 2	70	68	50	– 2	– 20
External rot.	50	78	81	+ 28	+ 31	82	77	75	– 5	– 7

Upper extremity strength

Table 2 lists arm and hand strength for the affected and unaffected arms pre-training (A1), post-training (A2) and follow-up (A3). All ten strength measures improved or remained the same as compared to A1. At follow-up, the gains in grip strength compared to pre-training were 231.3 N and 97.9N for the affected and unaffected hands, respectively. These results are 200% to 400% the MCID of 49 N for hand grip (20). At follow-up, the affected and unaffected hand two-finger pinch improved 29.8 N and 20.0 N, respectively and the 3-jaw pinch improved 36.5N for both hands, compared to pre-training. The affected shoulder strength had an impressive gain from 4.4N at A1 to 31.1N at A3, a 700% increase. The unaffected shoulder strength improvement was from 31.1N to 44.5N represents a more modest 40% increase.

Table 2. Hand and arm strength for the post-surgery cancer survivor experiencing chronic pain. © Bright Cloud International Corp. Reprinted by permission

	Affected Shoulder					Unaffected Shoulder				
Variable	A1	A2	A3	A2-A1	A3-A1	A1	A2	A3	A2-A1	A3-A1
Hand Grip	68	262.4	299.4	+194.4	+231.3	115.7	218.0	213.5	+102.3	+97.9
Tip Pinch	0.0	31.1	29.8	+31.1	+29.8	11.1	23.6	31.1	+12.5	+20.0
3 Jaw Pinch	4.4	46.7	40.9	+42.3	+36.5	16.9	34.7	53.4	+17.8	+36.5
Ant. Deltoid	4.4	22.2	31.1	+17.8	+26.7	31.1	31.1	44.5	0.0	+13.3
Lat. Deltoid	4.4	22.2	31.1	+17.8	+26.7	31.1	31.1	44.5	0.0	+13.3

Upper extremity functional assessments

Functional assessments also improved at post-training (A2) and follow-up (A3) relative to pre-training (A1). Fugl-Meyer Assessment scores were 47 (A1), 58 (A2) and 56 (A3). The 11 and 9 point improvement at A2 and A3 respectively meet the MCID criteria of 9 points (21). CAHAI-9 scores were 50 (A1), 63 (A2) and 63 (A3). The improvement of 13 points at A2 and A3 is twice the MCID of 6.3 points (22), and is indicative of improved ability to perform bimanual ADLs. The metric UEFI-20 measurements were 18 (A1), 58 (A2) and 42 (A3). The improvement of 40 and 24 points at A2 and A3 were three to five times the MCID of 8 points (13). The JHFT for the affected hand was 79 (A1), 35 (A2) and 39 (A3) seconds. The subject was able to complete the manual tasks of JHFT in half the time post-training, and the speed improvement was maintained at follow-up.

Cognitive and emotive outcomes

Table 3 lists emotive and cognitive measures evaluated pre-training, post-training and follow-up. There was a notable reduction in depression severity of 16 points (A2) and 6 points (A3). Both values were above MCID of 5 points for BDI-II (23). The Trail Making Test Part B showed a reduction in time from 128 seconds at A1 to 49 seconds at A3. This was indicative of improved attention and processing speed. HVLT-R which measures verbal learning and memory was one cognitive measure that showed a systematic decline from 22 points at A1, to 20 points at A2, and 16 points at A3. This was offset by an increase in word generation from 5 at A1, to 6 at A2 and 9 at A3. There was a systematic increase BVMT-R, from 13 points at A1, to 18 points at A2 and 20 points at A3, indicative of improved visuo-spatial memory.

Table 3. Emotive and cognitive outcomes for the post-surgery cancer survivor experiencing chronic pain. *indicates sign reversed so all positive differences in table indicates improvement. © Bright Cloud International Corp. Reprinted by permission

Variable	A1	A2	A3	A2-A1	A3-A1	Variable	A1	A2	A3	A2-A1	A3-A1
BDI-II	37	21	31	*+ 16	* + 6	HVLT-R	22	20	16	− 2	− 6
TMT-A	20	22	22	* − 2	* − 2	BVMT-R	13	18	20	+ 5	+ 7
TMT-B	128	66	49	* + 62	* +79	Word Gen	5	6	9	+ 1	+ 4

Subject Attendance and Testimonial

The subject completed the 16 sessions of the protocol over a period of nine weeks. She postponed two sessions early on due to back pain related to work and unrelated to BrightArm training. She reported no side-effects from the VR therapy such as cyber sickness or headache. The subject evaluated the system by answering the ten questions. The average response was 3.6/5 at the two sampling times (week 4 and week 8). The lowest scores were for the questions: "I had no pain or discomfort in my upper body?" (1.5), "Playing games with my affected arm(s) was easy?" (2.0), "I would encourage others to used it?" (3.0), "The length of the exercising in a day was appropriate?" (3.5). The responses averaged a rating of 4 between week 4 and 8 for the questions: "The system was easy to use, "Playing games with both arms was easy?," "There were few technical problems?," "Instructions given to me were useful?." The highest evaluation score was 5.0/5 for the questions: "I was not bored while exercising?" and "I liked the system overall?" which shows excellent technology acceptance of the BrightArm Duo.

At follow-up (A3) the subject was asked if she would provide a testimonial. In compliance to IRB Human Subject's Regulations her identity is not disclosed, although she included her name in the email sent in late May 2015. This email is included here with subject's approval, as it provides her opinion on the impact that the experimental therapy had on her life.

> "*I've just completed my 8 weeks of physical therapy. This therapy section helped me tremendously. Before I started this therapy my right arm had no use me and there was so much pain! There were things I couldn't do like driving, getting dressed, taking a shower, playing with my nephew....I was working on and off, I couldn't hang out with my friends, my life basically stopped, and it was very depressing. But now I'm driving, I'm back working full time, I'm catching up with friends AND there's no pain. I'm extremely happy with the results, this is my third time trying therapy for my arm and this the only one I saw results from. The therapy sessions consist of games....yes you are literally sitting in a chair in front of a computer playing games, though they were challenging it was also very fun, well for me it was. Dr. Burdea and his team gave me back my life because I thought it was over literally. I recommend everyone that's having this problem to try this therapy session, it works tremendously and it is fun (did I mention it's actually games you play on a computer) yes and everyone is very friendly. So thank you Bright Cloud International.*"

The subject was referring to BrightArm Duo in the physical therapy reported in this testimonial. She has compared VR games to the traditional physical therapy she had undergone in the past which did not work for her. The immersive games induced bilateral high repetitions and engaged the participant with rewarding feedback for effort. These features made the rehabilitation training with BrightArm Duo distinctly different from her prior traditional therapy.

DISCUSSION

Childhood cancer survivors have an increased risk of complications later in life and rehabilitation with better outcomes will greatly improve the quality of life in these women (24). In this study, the 22-year old female subject showed marked reduction in shoulder and arm pain of 4.4 points on the NRS scale which is much higher than the MCID of 2.17 for NRS established for people with surgical and post-surgical shoulder pain (25). This is an encouraging finding considering the impact of VR therapy on chronic pain in other conditions such as fibromyalgia has shown no benefits for pain intensity (26). However, the benefits of VR therapy in cancer related pain during acute painful procedures, hospitalization and chemotherapy has been studied and shown to be beneficial (27). Visual distraction has been one of the theories put forth for explaining these beneficial effects on pain (6). Although, in this study, the positive effect on pain intensity cannot be completely attributed to the phenomenon of visual distraction. As reported in literature (28), the distraction from pain could be insufficient to cause the accompanied improvements on motor and cognitive aspects of function measured at post-training and maintained at 8-week follow up. It is also likely that the 16-session protocol used in this study resulted in better outcomes than the 10-session protocol reported in other studies of VR in chronic pain of fibromyalgia (29).

Garcia-Palacios et al. (26) reported no benefit of VR therapy on depression in people with chronic pain due to fibromyalgia, whereas in this study, the depression scores decreased by 16 points on the BDI-II, which is a 32% improvement. The MCID for depression varies with initial severity (30) and has been estimated to be 32% for individuals with prolonged depression which fits the profile of the subject in this study. A recent review by Chirico et al. (27) summarizes the benefit of VR therapy in cancer on psychological variables such as state anxiety and painful procedures, the results of the present case study open the possibility to understand the impact of VR therapy in other variables such as depression. They also recommend including bio physiological variables in VR therapy research in cancer using biosensors for understanding physiological responses to the training. In this study, biosensors at the wrist of the unaffected arm showed a 10.25°F increase in skin temperature with the over the course of the 16 sessions conducted in the same indoor therapy room. This interesting finding is indicative of an increased thermal response during exercise that is likely during moderate to high intensity exercise (31) and was associated with improved outcomes in the subject. This may indicate increased blood flow to the arm with a beneficial effect for overall health of the arm (32).

An average of 1,260 active arm repetitions and 440 hand grasps per session for the subject over the course of 16 sessions is an important characteristic of the BrightArm Duo therapy. This large number of induced arm repetitions has previously been reported (7) to benefit elderly stroke survivors in the chronic phase. The substantial benefits of this intensive therapy are indicative of application for chronic cancer pain populations as well. All standardized measures in this case study of range of motion, strength, UE function, attention, and memory improved at post-training. With the NRS pain level of 6 and 7 pre-training, the subject was unable to move her right arm and post training the regained range of motion in the arm along with simultaneous distraction from pain has shown to be the right combination of therapy for her. As seen from her own testimonial, the subject was able to transition to a full time job and returned to driving giving her maximal functional independence much desired at her young age.

A remarkable finding in this case study was that at 8-week follow up (A3) the majority of gains remained higher than A1, with no VR training for eight weeks (after A2). The subject did not report playing any form of videogames during the no-VR phase and enjoyed reading and socializing for recreation. The maintenance effect with VR therapy has been shown in prior studies in 48 hour follow-up (5), however, to the authors' knowledge, a 8-week follow up has not been reported previously. The study of VR maintenance effect for rehabilitation therapy programs is as critical for chronic pain conditions as it is for rehabilitation of conditions such as stroke. This case study is supportive of the feasibility of a longitudinal study protocol to study these maintenance effects of VR therapy in chronic pain and depression.

This study, part of an n=6 feasibility evaluation of the BrightArm Duo system for upper body chronic pain, has obvious limitations to generalizability. However, the information detailed in this case study brings forth the qualitative aspects associated with BrightArm Duo training especially in younger individuals and helps examine the feasibility of the VR therapy in this sample of cancer survivors. The therapists can benefit from an in-depth study of successful cases using BrightArm Duo system in rehabilitation to maximize benefits for their clients. In conclusion, initial findings demonstrate a meaningful reduction in chronic pain and physical, cognitive and psychological improvement for a young female subject. These outcomes suggest a need for controlled studies in young subjects with pain and depression associated to post-surgical treatment of breast cancer.

ACKNOWLEDGMENTS

Research reported here was supported by grant 1R43DA032224-01 from the National Institutes for Health/NIDA. We wish to thank Abby Eisner OT and Daniel Saldana who performed the clinical evaluations and Ms. Noreen Rana, the clinical coordinator for the study.

REFERENCES

[1] Zebrack BJ. Psychological, social, and behavioral issues for young adults with cancer. *Cancer* 2011;117(10 Suppl):2289–94.

[2] Quinn GP, Gonçalves V, Sehovic I, Bowman ML, Reed DR. Quality of life in adolescent and young adult cancer patients: a systematic review of the literature. *Patient Relat Outcome Meas* 2015;6:19–51.

[3] Kenyon M, Mayer D, Owens A. Late and long-term effects of breast cancer treatment and surveillance management for the general practitioner. *J Obstet Gynecol Neonatal Nurs* 2014;43(3):382–98.

[4] Hoffman HG, Doctor JN, Patterson DR, Carrougher GJ, Furness TA3rd. Virtual reality as an adjunctive pain control during burn wound care in adolescent patients. *Pain* 2000;85(1-2):305–9.

[5] Schneider S, Ellis M, Coombs W, Shonkwiler E, Folsom L. Virtual reality intervention for older women with breast cancer. *Cyberpsychol Behav* 2003;6(3):301–7.

[6] Triberti S, Repetto C, Riva G. Psychological factors influencing the effectiveness of virtual reality-based analgesia: a systematic review. *Cyberpsychol Behav Soc Netw* 2014;17(6):335–45.

[7] House G, Burdea G, Polistico K, Roll D, Kim J, Grampurohit N, et al. Integrative rehabilitation of residents chronic post-stroke in skilled nursing facilities: the design and evaluation of the BrightArm Duo. *Disabil Rehabil Assist Technol* 2016;11(8):683-94.

[8] Unity Technologies. Unity Manual. URL: http://docs.unity3d.com/Manual/index.html.

[9] Paice JA, Cohen FL. Validity of a verbally administered numeric rating scale to measure cancer pain intensity. *Cancer Nurs* 1997;20(2):88–93.

[10] Duncan PW, Propst M, Nelson SG. Reliability of the Fugl-Meyer assessment of sensorimotor recovery following cerebrovascular accident. Phys Ther 1983;63(10):1606–10.

[11] Barreca S, Gowland C, Stratford P, Huijbregts M, Griffiths J, Torresin W, et al. Development of the Chedoke Arm and Hand Activity Inventory: theoretical constructs, item generation, and selection. *Top Stroke Rehabil* 2004;11(4):31–42.

[12] Jebsen RH, Taylor N, Trieschmann RB, Trotter MJ, Howard LA. An objective and standardized test of hand function. *Arch Phys Med Rehabil* 1969;50(6):311–9.

[13] Chesworth B, Hamilton C, Walton D, Benoit M, Blake TA, Bredy H, et al. Reliability and validity of two versions of the upper extremity functional index. *Physiother Can* 2014;66(3):243–53.

[14] Beck A, Steer R, Brown G. Manual for Beck Depression Inventory, 2nd ed. Antonio, TX: Psychology Corp, 1996.

[15] White T, Stern R. Neuropsychological Assessment Battery. Lutz, FL: Psychological Assessment Resources 2003.

[16] Brandt J, Benedict R. Hopkins Verbal Learning Test Revised. Lutz, FL: Psychological Assessment Resources, 2001.

[17] Benedict R. Brief Visuospatial Memory Test Revised. Odessa, FL: Psychological Assessment Resources, 1997.

[18] Reitan R. Validity of the Trail Making Test as an indicator of organic brain damage. *Percept Motor Skills* 1958;8:271–6.

[19] Salamh P, Kolber M. The reliability, minimal detectable change and construct validity of a clinical measurement for quantifying posterior shoulder tightness in the post-operative population. *Int J Sports PhysTher*, 2012:7(6), 565–75.

[20] Lang CE, Edwards DF, Birkenmeier RL, Dromerick AW. Estimating minimal clinically important differences of upper-extremity measures early after stroke. *Arch Phys Med Rehabil*, 2008:89(9), 1693–1700.

[21] Arya KN, Verma R, Garg RK. Estimating the minimal clinically important difference of an upper extremity recovery measure in subacute stroke patients. *Top Stroke Rehabil*, 18 Suppl 1, 2011:599–610.

[22] Barreca SR. *Chedoke Arm and Hand Activity Inventory (CAHAI).* 2015, from http://www.cahai.ca/manual.html

[23] Hiroe T, Kojima M, Yamamoto I, Nojima S, Kinoshita Y, Hashimoto N, et al. Gradations of clinical severity and sensitivity to change assessed with the Beck Depression Inventory-II in Japanese patients with depression. *Psychiatry Res*, 2005:135(3), 229–35.

[24] Kenney LB, Yasui Y, Inskip PD, Hammond S, Neglia JP, Mertens AC, et al. Breast cancer after childhood cancer: a report from the Childhood Cancer Survivor Study. *Ann Intern Med* 2004;141(8):590–97.

[25] Michener L, Snyder A, Leggin B. Responsiveness of the numeric pain rating scale in patients with shoulder pain and the effect of surgical status. *J Sport Rehabil* 2011;20(1):115–28.

[26] Garcia-Palacios A, Herrero R, Vizcaino Y, Belmonte MA, Castilla D, Molinari, et al. Integrating virtual reality with activity management for the treatment of fibromyalgia: acceptability and preliminary efficacy. *Clin J Pain* 2015;31(6):564–72.

[27] Chirico A, Lucidi F, De Laurentiis M, Milanese C, Napoli A, Giordano A. Virtual reality in health system: Beyond entertainment. A mini-review on the efficacy of VR during cancer treatment. *J Cell Physiol* 2016;231(2):275–87.

[28] Loreto-Quijada, D, Gutiérrez-Maldonado J, Nieto R, Gutierrez-Martinez O, Ferrer-Garcia M, Saldana C, et al. Differential effects of two virtual reality interventions: distraction versus pain control. *Cyberpsychology Behav Soc Netw* 2014;17(6):353–8.

[29] Botella C, Garcia-Palacios A, Vizcaíno Y, Herrero R, Banos RM, Belmonte MA. Virtual reality in the treatment of fibromyalgia: a pilot study. *Cyberpsychol Behav Soc Netw* 2013;16(3):215–23.

[30] Button KS, Kounali D, Thomas L, Wiles NJ, Peters TJ, Welton NJ, et al. Minimal clinically important difference on the Beck Depression Inventory--II according to the patient's perspective. *Psychological Med*, 2015:45(15), 3269–79.

[31] Neves E, Vilaca-Alves J, Antunes N. Felisberto IM, Rosa C, Reis VM. Different responses of the skin temperature to physical exercise: Systematic review. Conference *Proc IEEE Eng Med Biol SocAnn Conf*, 2015:1307–10.

SECTION TWO: ACKNOWLEDGMENTS

In: Rehabilitation
Editors: Wendy Powell et al.
ISBN: 978-1-53612-080-6

Chapter 13

ABOUT THE EDITORS

Wendy A Powell, PhD is a Reader in Virtual Reality and leads the Virtual Interaction and Applications (VIA) research group at the University of Portsmouth School of Creative Technologies. She is also Deputy Director of the Centre for Health Modeling and Informatics. Wendy initially trained as a chiropractor and worked for many years in clinical practice before undertaking a degree in computer science and a PhD in creative technologies. For the past 12 years she has conducted research on the ways in which virtual reality system interactions affect perception and behaviour, with a particular focus on the implications for virtual rehabilitation. She works in both fundamental and applied research, and has been involved in VR projects across a wide range of clinical applications including phantom limb pain in amputees, dementia support, stroke rehabilitation and hospital infection control. In 2015 Wendy was elevated to Senior Membership of the Institute of Electrical and Electronics Engineers (IEEE) in recognition of her technical and professional excellence, and she regularly represents the IEEE to the media and industry as a technical expert in virtual reality. Email: wendy.powell@port.ac.uk

Albert "Skip" Rizzo, PhD is a clinical psychologist and Director of Medical Virtual Reality at the University of Southern California Institute for

Creative Technologies. He is also a Research Professor with the USC Department of Psychiatry and at the USC Davis School of Gerontology. Over the last 20 years, Skip has conducted research on the design, development and evaluation of Virtual Reality systems targeting the areas of clinical assessment, treatment and rehabilitation across the domains of psychological, cognitive and motor functioning in both healthy and clinical populations. This work has focused on PTSD, TBI, autism, ADHD, Alzheimer's disease, stroke and other clinical conditions. In spite of the diversity of these clinical R&D areas, the common thread that drives all of his work with digital technologies involves the study of how interactive and immersive Virtual Reality simulations can be usefully applied to address human healthcare needs beyond what is possible with traditional 20th Century tools and methods. Email: rizzo@ict.usc.edu

Paul M Sharkey, HDipEE, BSc(Eng), MA, PhD, is a professor emeritus of the University of Reading, United Kingdom, having retired as professor of cybernetics, member of the Cybernetics Research Group and Director of the Visualisation and Interactive Technologies Centre at the School of Systems Engineering, University of Reading, Reading. Professor Sharkey's research interests lie in the fields of robotics, control systems, active vision and virtual reality, particularly in the overlapping areas within these fields relating to systems architecture and systems where delays are an inherent part of the closed loop. In 1996 he founded, and remains the Programme Chair for, the International Conference Series on Disability, Virtual Reality and Associated Technologies, a biennial conference that brings together psychologists, physical and occupational therapists, clinicians, engineers and computer scientists to further understanding in the multi-disciplinary area in the field of rehabilitation and disability. He was also a founding member and is a current member of the Board of Directors for the International Society for Virtual Rehabilitation. In 2010, he was elected a Fellow of the Intstitution of Engineering and Technology. Email: p.m.sharkey@reading.ac.uk

Joav Merrick, MD, MMedSci, DMSc, born and educated in Denmark is professor of pediatrics, child health and human development, Division of Pediatrics, Hadassah Hebrew University Medical Center, Mt Scopus Campus, Jerusalem, Israel and Kentucky Children's Hospital, University of Kentucky, Lexington, Kentucky United States and professor of public health at the Center for Healthy Development, School of Public Health, Georgia State University, Atlanta, United States, the medical director of the Health Services, Division for Intellectual and Developmental Disabilities, Ministry of Social Affairs and Social Services, Jerusalem, the founder and director of the National Institute of Child Health and Human Development in Israel. Numerous publications in the field of pediatrics, child health and human development, rehabilitation, intellectual disability, disability, health, welfare, abuse, advocacy, quality of life and prevention. Received the Peter Sabroe Child Award for outstanding work on behalf of Danish Children in 1985 and the International LEGO-Prize ("The Children's Nobel Prize") for an extraordinary contribution towards improvement in child welfare and well-being in 1987. Email: jmerrick@zahav.net.il

In: Rehabilitation
Editors: Wendy Powell et al.
ISBN: 978-1-53612-080-6

Chapter 14

About the School of Creative Technologies, University of Portsmouth, United Kingdom

The University of Portsmouth is rated in the top 2% of the World's Universities and is one of the top 150 Universities under 50 years old (Times Higher Education World University Rankings). The University is based in the island City of Portsmouth, with a rich maritime history and an abundance of cultural and waterfront attractions

The School of Creative Technologies was established in 2002 to act as a focus for the development of technical excellence and innovation in animation, computer games, film and broadcasting, music and sound and web/mobile applications with a strong multi-disciplinary, industry-led, vocational ethos. The School of Creative Technologies has grown to 60 academics and over 1,300 students, with most of the staff having real industry experience and excellent links with the creative industries.

Virtual reality (VR) is one of the new technologies at the core of our research focus, and the VIA (virtual interactions and applications) Research group has developed a strong international reputation in both technical and applied virtual reality, studying both the application of VR to a range of disciplines (such as healthcare and heritage) and also the fundamental effect of the user interaction within a VR environment. The group works closely with clinicians, industry and third sector organisations both locally and internationally, and also boasts a vibrant community of post-graduate research students.

Contact

Wendy Powell, PhD, Reader in Virtual Reality
School of Creative Technologies
University of Portsmouth, Eldon Building
Winston Churchill Avenue
Portsmouth PO1 2DJ
United Kingdom
Email: wendy.powell@port.ac.uk

In: Rehabilitation
Editors: Wendy Powell et al.
ISBN: 978-1-53612-080-6

Chapter 15

About the Institute for Creative Technologies (ICT)

The University of Southern California (USC), Institute for Creative Technologies (ICT) is an award-winning research center that advances the state-of-the-art in virtual reality (VR) and immersive environments. In 1999, the United States Army awarded ICT the largest research contract in USC history with the primary aim of developing VR simulation tools for general and tactical military training needs. This funding has brought together an interdisciplinary talent pool from academia, the entertainment industry, and the military. ICT is home to world class academic talent which is represented by a number of USC schools, including the School of Cinema-TV, the School of Engineering and its Information Sciences Institute (ISI) and Integrated Media Systems Center (IMSC), Keck School of Medicine, and the Annenberg School for Communication. Meanwhile, the entertainment industry brings creative talent from the entertainment and game development industries with expertise in visual effects, gaming, story, character, and production to the Institute.

This interdisciplinary academic Institute has produced leading edge research on simulation technologies such as artificial intelligence, graphics, interface and display technology and immersive audio. No other laboratory in the world has such ready access to world class talent across the range of disciplines that impact virtual human design: Computer graphics, computer animation, computer games, audio rendering, artificial intelligence, natural language processing, and Hollywood/game industry professional content producers (graphic artists, CGI animators, audio engineers, writers, actors, etc.).

Contact

Albert "Skip" Rizzo, PhD
Director, Medical Virtual Reality, Institute for Creative Technologies
Research Professor, Department of Psychiatry and School of Gerontology
University of Southern California
12015 East Waterfront Dr, Playa Vista, CA 90094, United States
Email: rizzo@ict.usc.edu
Please check out (and share) our crowd funding site to build a Virtual Vietnam PTSD treatment tool: https://ignite.usc.edu/project/480
ICT MedVR: http://medvr.ict.usc.edu/
Check out our work on YouTube:
http://www.youtube.com/user/AlbertSkipRizzo

In: Rehabilitation
Editors: Wendy Powell et al.
ISBN: 978-1-53612-080-6

Chapter 16

ABOUT THE UNIVERSITY OF READING, UNITED KINGDOM

The University of Reading is ranked amongst the United Kingdoms's highly research-intensive universities and within the top 250 universities in the world. It enjoys a world-class reputation for teaching, research and enterprise. Established as an extension college of Christ Church, Oxford in 1892, the University received a Royal Charter in 1926, the only university to do so between the two world wars. Important achievements include being the first university to win the Queen's Award for Export Achievement (1989) and on three occassions received the Queen's Anniversary Prize for Higher Education (1998, 2006 and 2009).

The quality and diversity of the research at Reading is recognised nationally and internationally. Reading is home to several centres of excellence and conducts world-class research across a broad range of disciplines. The UK's Research Excellence Framework (REF) latest results confirm the standing of the University of Reading as within the top 20 of the UK's research-intensive universities. Published in December 2014, the outcomes recognise the University research as being 78% 'internationally excellent', over one third of which is classes as 'world leading', ranking the Univeristy 19th in the UK in terms of research intensity. The work of over 600 University of Reading research active staff was submitted to the Higher

Education Funding Council for England for the RAE (88% of our eligible staff), demonstrating the breadth and quality of research across the university. In February 2015, the University or Reading was awarded the the European Commission's HR Excellence in Research Award.

Beyond research, one of the University's greatest attractions is its magnificent setting. Many hectares of mature parkland provide the backdrop to an interesting mix of traditional and modern architecture to create a unique campus atmosphere. This peaceful 130 hectare country estate, with its conservation meadows, rare tree collection and large lake, is an exceptional place to study, live and work.

Contact

Paul M Sharkey, HDipEE, BSc(Eng), MA, PhD
Professor emeritus
University of Reading
Whiteknights, Reading, RG6 6AY, United Kingdom
Email: p.m.sharkey@reading.ac.uk

In: Rehabilitation
Editors: Wendy Powell et al.
ISBN: 978-1-53612-080-6

Chapter 17

About the National Institute of Child Health and Human Development in Israel

The National Institute of Child Health and Human Development (NICHD) in Israel was established in 1998 as a virtual institute under the auspices of the Medical Director, Ministry of Social Affairs and Social Services in order to function as the research arm for the Office of the Medical Director. In 1998 the National Council for Child Health and Pediatrics, Ministry of Health and in 1999 the Director General and Deputy Director General of the Ministry of Health endorsed the establishment of the NICHD.

Mission

The mission of a National Institute for Child Health and Human Development in Israel is to provide an academic focal point for the scholarly interdisciplinary study of child life, health, public health, welfare, disability, rehabilitation, intellectual disability and related aspects of human development. This mission includes research, teaching, clinical work, information and public service activities in the field of child health and human development.

Service and academic activities

Over the years many activities became focused in the south of Israel due to collaboration with various professionals at the Faculty of Health Sciences (FOHS) at the Ben Gurion University of the Negev (BGU). Since 2000 an affiliation with the Zusman Child Development Center at the Pediatric Division of Soroka University Medical Center has resulted in collaboration around the establishment of the Down Syndrome Clinic at that center. In 2002 a full course on "Disability" was established at the Recanati School for Allied Professions in the Community, FOHS, BGU and in 2005 collaboration was started with the Primary Care Unit of the faculty and disability became part of the master of public health course on "Children and society". In the academic year 2005-2006 a one semester course on "Aging with disability" was started as part of the master of science program in gerontology in our collaboration with the Center for Multidisciplinary Research in Aging. In 2010 collaborations with the Division of Pediatrics, Hadassah Hebrew University Medical Center, Jerusalem, Israel around the National Down Syndrome Center and teaching students and residents about intellectual and developmental disabilities as part of their training at this campus.

Research activities

The affiliated staff have over the years published work from projects and research activities in this national and international collaboration. In the year 2000 the International Journal of Adolescent Medicine and Health and in 2005 the International Journal on Disability and Human Development of De Gruyter Publishing House (Berlin and New York) were affiliated with the

National Institute of Child Health and Human Development. From 2008 also the International Journal of Child Health and Human Development (Nova Science, New York), the International Journal of Child and Adolescent Health (Nova Science) and the Journal of Pain Management (Nova Science) affiliated and from 2009 the International Public Health Journal (Nova Science) and Journal of Alternative Medicine Research (Nova Science). All peer-reviewed international journals.

National collaborations

Nationally the NICHD works in collaboration with the Faculty of Health Sciences, Ben Gurion University of the Negev; Department of Physical Therapy, Sackler School of Medicine, Tel Aviv University; Autism Center, Assaf HaRofeh Medical Center; National Rett and PKU Centers at Chaim Sheba Medical Center, Tel HaShomer; Department of Physiotherapy, Haifa University; Department of Education, Bar Ilan University, Ramat Gan, Faculty of Social Sciences and Health Sciences; College of Judea and Samaria in Ariel and in 2011 affiliation with Center for Pediatric Chronic Diseases and National Center for Down Syndrome, Department of Pediatrics, Hadassah Hebrew University Medical Center, Mount Scopus Campus, Jerusalem.

International collaborations

Internationally with the Department of Disability and Human Development, College of Applied Health Sciences, University of Illinois at Chicago; Strong Center for Developmental Disabilities, Golisano Children's Hospital at Strong, University of Rochester School of Medicine and Dentistry, New York; Centre on Intellectual Disabilities, University of Albany, New York; Centre for Chronic Disease Prevention and Control, Health Canada, Ottawa; Chandler Medical Center and Children's Hospital, Kentucky Children's

Hospital, Section of Adolescent Medicine, University of Kentucky, Lexington; Chronic Disease Prevention and Control Research Center, Baylor College of Medicine, Houston, Texas; Division of Neuroscience, Department of Psychiatry, Columbia University, New York; Institute for the Study of Disadvantage and Disability, Atlanta; Center for Autism and Related Disorders, Department Psychiatry, Children's Hospital Boston, Boston; Department of Pediatric and Adolescent Medicine, Western Michigan University Homer Stryker MD School of Medicine, Kalamazoo, Michigan, United States; Department of Paediatrics, Child Health and Adolescent Medicine, Children's Hospital at Westmead, Westmead, Australia; International Centre for the Study of Occupational and Mental Health, Düsseldorf, Germany; Centre for Advanced Studies in Nursing, Department of General Practice and Primary Care, University of Aberdeen, Aberdeen, United Kingdom; Quality of Life Research Center, Copenhagen, Denmark; Nordic School of Public Health, Gottenburg, Sweden, Scandinavian Institute of Quality of Working Life, Oslo, Norway; The Department of Applied Social Sciences (APSS) of The Hong Kong Polytechnic University Hong Kong.

Targets

Our focus is on research, international collaborations, clinical work, teaching and policy in health, disability and human development and to establish the NICHD as a permanent institute in Israel in order to conduct model research and together with the four university schools of public health/medicine in Israel establish a national master and doctoral program in disability and human development at the institute to secure the next generation of professionals working in this often non-prestigious/low-status field of work.

Contact

Joav Merrick, MD, MMedSci, DMSc
Professor of Pediatrics
Medical Director, Health Services, Division for Intellectual and Developmental Disabilities, Ministry of Social Affairs and Social Services, POB 1260, IL-91012 Jerusalem, Israel.
E-mail: jmerrick@zahav.net.il

In: Rehabilitation
Editors: Wendy Powell et al.
ISBN: 978-1-53612-080-6

Chapter 18

About the Book Series "Disability Studies"

Disability studies is a book series with publications from a multidisciplinary group of researchers, practitioners and clinicians for an international professional forum interested in the broad spectrum of disability, intellectual disability, health and human development.

- Reiter S. Disability from a humanistic perspective: Towards a better quality of life. New York: Nova Science, 2008
- Knotkova H, Cruciani R, Merrick J, eds. Pain. Brain stimulation in the treatment of pain. New York: Nova Science, 2010.
- Prasher VP, ed. Contemporary issues in intellectual disabilities. New York: Nova Science, 2010.
- Lotan M, Merrick J, eds. Rett syndrome: Therapeutic interventions. New York: Nova Science, 2011.
- Satgé D, Merrick J, eds. Cancer in children and adults with intellectual disabilities: Current research aspects. New York: Nova Science, 2011.
- Knotkova H, Cruciani RA, Merrick J, eds. Neural plasticity in chronic pain. New York: Nova Science, 2011.
- Prasher VP. Down syndrome and dementia. A comprehensive and historical review. New York: Nova Science, 2012.

- Merrick J, Aspler S, Morad M, eds. Disability and chronic disease. New York: Nova Science, 2013.
- Tse MMY, Merrick J. Pain and the elderly. New York: Nova Science, 2013.
- Brown RI, Faragher RM, eds. Quality of life and intellectuall disability: Knowledge application to other social and educational challenges. New York: Nova Science, 2014.
- Grenon I. From one century to the next: A history of Wrentham State School and the Institutional Model in Massachusetts. New York: Nova Science, 2014.
- Sharkey PM, Merrick J, eds. Virtual reality: People with special needs. New York: Nova Science, 2014.
- Sharkey PM, Merrick J, eds. Virtual reality: Rehabilitation in motor, cognitive and sensorial disorders. New York: Nova Science, 2014.
- Merrick J, Greydanus DE, Patel DR, eds. Intellectual disability: Some current issues New York: Nova Science, 2014.
- Pareto L, Sharkey PM, Merrick J, eds. Technology, rehabilitation and empowerment of people with special needs. New York: Nova Science, 2015.
- Sharkey PM, Merrick J, eds. Recent advances on using virtual reality technologies for rehabilitation. New York: Nova Science, 2016.
- Omar HA, Patel DR, Greydanus DE, Merrick J, eds. Pediatric pain: Current aspects. New York: Nova Science, 2016.

Contact

Professor Joav Merrick, MD, MMedSci, DMSc

Medical Director, Health Services, Division for Intellectual and Developmental Disabilities, Ministry of Social Affairs and Social Services, POBox 1260

IL-91012 Jerusalem, Israel

E-mail: jmerrick@internet-zahav.net

SECTION THREE: INDEX

INDEX

B

C

D

E

F

G

H

I

J

K

L

M

Q

R

S

T

U

V

W

Y